Haile Gebrselassie

The Greatest Runner of All Time

Klaus Weidt

Haile Gebrselassie

The Greatest Runner of All Time

Meyer & Meyer Sport

This book is dedicated to all keen endurance runners, either marathon runners or casual runners. "Everyone who overcomes himself for his own enjoyment, health or for a competition is a winner," says Haile Gebrselassie and talking about himself: "I will always run, even when I'm no longer interested in records and medals. For running is life."

The author thanks all those who have supported him. Particularly Haile Gebrselassie himself, Ethiopian friends Amanuel Hawariat, Coach Dr. Yilma Berta and Andulem Tesfaw. A big thank you also Lutz Kuhardt who actively supported him in the preparation of this book.

He found further information and tips in the following publications: "The Greatest" (breakaway books). "Running with Haile Gebrselassie" (Ehrenwirth, Verlagsgruppe Lubbe). "Paul Tergat" (Meyer & Meyer Sport), "Äthiopien" (Reise Know How), "Äthiopien" (Nelles Verlag).

Original title: Haile Gebrselassie – Auf den Spuren einer Lauflegende

Translated by Heather Ross

British Library Cataloguing in Publication Data
A catalogue record for this book is available from the British Library

Haile Gebrselassie – The Greatest Runner of All Time
Klaus Weidt
Maidenhead: Meyer & Meyer Sport (UK) Ltd., 2011
ISBN: 978-1-84126-323-6

Auckland, Beirut, Budapest, Cairo, Cape Town, Dubai, Graz, Indianapolis, Maidenhead, Melbourne, Olten, Singapore, Tehran, Toronto
Member of the World
Sport Publishers' Association (WSPA)
www.w-s-p-a.org
Printed by: B.O.S.S Druck und Medien GmbH
ISBN: 978-1-84126-323-6
E-Mail: info@m-m-sports.com
www.m-m-sports.com

Contents

1 In Search of Haile

How do you get an Ethiopian vest number?

I got to know him personally quite late. I had, of course, followed his progress from the start and been amazed at his records and victories, which fell like apples from the trees with not a bad one among them. I was not the only one to think he was like an extraterrestrial among endurance athletes, although history told us that Africa's running stars had already achieved many stellar performances. Abebe Bikila springs to mind. However, the number of medals that Haile Gebrselassie, this young man from ancient Ethiopia, has collected, was astonishing. Journalists' accolades piled up, from "runner of the century" to "running prodigy."

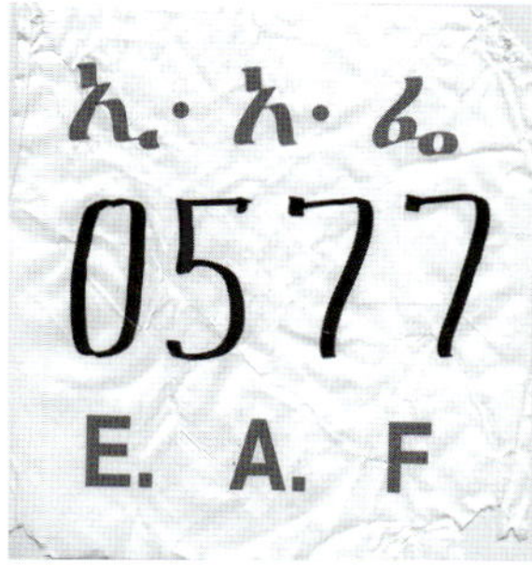

The author's vest number in the Abebe-Bikila Marathon 2005.

My desire to meet him in person could not be fulfilled either at World Championships, Olympic Games or record-breaking performances. Haile always disappears as quickly as he arrives. A comet. Press conferences that he admittedly presented with his incomparable smile and unfailing humor, could only give a small insight into his life. How could I enter it though, to get to know more about him and his life?

According to my research, no German running group had ever been to the land of Haile Gebrselassie and Abebe Bikila to race in a Marathon. The Ethiopian stars deliberately fly, like their Kenyan neighbors, to selected European races, tempted by big prize money, which, when one knows the lifestyles of these African regions, is quite understandable. So, we really wanted to travel to this east African high country between Sudan, Somalia and Kenya, not far from

Haile Gebrselassie with Amanual Hawariat, who made it possible for German guests to take part in this Marathon race for the first time, previously reserved for African talent-spotting.

HAILE GEBRSELASSIE

View over part of verdant Addis Ababa.

the Horn of Africa, with its fascinating landscapes and historically rich cultures.

But how?

Two Ethiopian travel firms were set a seemingly impossible task. They had to find out when and where a local Marathon race would take place and whether Haile Gebrselassie would be in town at the time. Both gave themselves a year to complete the task and – gave up. However, a Marathon was identified, it even had tradition and was usually held in June, in Addis Ababa. Already over two decades old, named for the Marathon legend Abebe Bikila, as a test race for all Ethiopians who wanted to emulate their successful running stars. There were usually at least 500 of them. I was surprised; this was very interesting and exciting. However, none of the country's sports leaders wanted to commit to an exact date and to pin down Gebrselassie to a specific time, making it all the more difficult to organize. "Sorry," these travel agencies eventually said, and let the business go.

However, I did manage to find a third one. At the International Tourism Fair in the Berlin Trade Fair halls at the Radio Tower, a dark-skinned young man with a mustache followed me around and spoke to me in fluent German: "Hallo, wollen Sie nicht mal nach Äthiopien?" (Hello would you like to go to Ethiopia?) He introduced himself as Amanuel, head of a tourism firm that he had founded after the painful realization after many years of studying shipping in Rostock (Germany) that he was in

Measuring 1.1 million km^2, situated in eastern Africa, the Federal Democratic Republic of Ethiopia is one of the largest countries on the continent. The culture and traditions of the ancient Abyssinians go back more than 3000 years. About 80 million inhabitants speak 83 languages and 200 dialects in this country, a region of contrasting landscapes from the highlands that rises to an altitude of over 14,750 feet, to the Great Rift Valley and the source of the blue Nile. 85% of the population are farmers. Ethiopians were never colonized. The native language is Amharic.

the wrong faculty. Eritrea, formerly part of Ethiopia, on the Red Sea, had declared independence.

Amanuel stuck to his guns, even when I told him about the resignation of his competitors. “Leave it to me, I can do it.“ I gave him just six months…

Amanuel really did it. Two months after our meeting, we received an email saying: Abebe-Bikila Marathon on June 8th, you can take part and Haile will also be in Addis. With typical ambition, he had convinced the Ethiopian Athletics Federation to let us attend and commit to an exact date. What I didn’t know was that he had admittedly not contacted Haile, but learnt from his secretary, that he had no overseas commitments in his diary on that date.

We were immediately enthusiastic and formed a running tour group, which eventually comprised two dozen people, including (the occasion was more than worth it) the Editors in Chief of two German running magazines. On June 5th, they all excitedly boarded the Ethiopian Airlines night flight.

Turbulence at 8,200 feet and a "detour"

The night flight was calm and the landing in Addis Ababa, the highest-altitude city in Africa, was smooth. Even the tourist coach was waiting at the airport on time, but Amanuel’s joy at our arrival could not hide some anxiety. There was turbulence at 8,200 feet. Had Haile flown out? Would the Marathon be postponed? Did the organizer ignore the fact that we also wanted to run a half Marathon?

What we had not realized in Germany was that serious unrest had broken out in the Ethiopian capital. The opposition powers challenged the freshly released election results and brought several thousand people onto the streets, who were soon confronted by armed police. The confrontation took not long to erupt, shots were fired and protesters were injured. Some newspapers even mentioned fatalities. We now found ourselves right in the middle of this dangerous situation.

Addis Ababa (‘new flower’ in Amharic) did not seem so colorful on the day of our arrival, but rather faded instead. Barely any cars could be seen on the wide streets, which was unusual for this busy capital city. The Bole Road, one of the busiest boulevards, was almost empty. Even the Alem Building, Haile Gebrselassie’s business tower block, looked deserted. Amanuel dialed Haile’s now familiar number on his cell phone but there was no answer. The several hundred stores in the rambling Merkato market, which is even bigger than the El-Khalili Bazaar in Cairo, were all shut.

It was little surprise that to start with we snuck out of this dangerous situation in Addis after only a short stay. We went on a two-day excursion into the 'Cradle of Life', as the hilly landscape to the Wenchi Crater, about 130 miles from the capital was called in the brochures. Of course, we had no objection to this, but pointed out that there were two events that we could not miss: running in the Abebe-Bikila Marathon, should it take place, and the meeting with Haile. What happened next put our minds at rest. The journey through the green expanses of southwestern Ethiopia and the straggling street villages were already exciting for us by itself. People in colorful or completely white clothing, barefoot or in light sandals, who seemed to all be moving in one direction for miles on end. With water pots or plastic containers on their heads, in their hands or, for those lucky enough, transported on their donkeys' backs. In between, we kept coming across herds of goats, cattle, and sheep that had right of way here. It was astonishing how the driver at the wheel of our mini-bus, through many years' training, managed to make the necessary dodging maneuvers so perfectly. Straw-covered clean huts, fertile highlands, to the right and left a well-asphalted highway funded with UN money, farmers on the fields plowing with their wooden equipment in a way that had not changed for many hundred years.

Waliso, also called Ghion, is situated in the Gurage Region, 80 miles southwest of Addis Ababa. The city has become a tourist destination due to its spa waters. From Waliso, the impressive Wenchi Crater can be visited. The Gurage tribe is famous in Ethiopia for its trading and farming skills.

Our destination, the city of Waliso, also known as Ghion, left an ambivalent impression. Between the cemented houses stood countless corrugated iron and mud huts in front of which a steady stream of business was carried on. On the bumpy and muddy road to our lodgings, it was almost impossible to pass through animals of all kinds, churchgoers and playing children. The running tour group grew quieter and quieter, the faces longer and longer. Is this where we were to stay the night? Then we entered a kind of paradise: a resort with bungalows, diverse plant life, monkeys, well-stocked gardens and a swimming pool. Ethiopia's new tourist destination for its foreign guests. We did not stay in this relaxing location, but quickly walked past the huts, were quite shocked at how simple they were, played table tennis with the children and were surprised that in spite of the great poverty there was a smile on every face. It was not like the slums that I had seen on the outskirts of Nairobi or Cape Town. There was no trash along the sides of the roads, no stinking sewage, although no sewage system existed.

Before we returned to Addis Ababa, we undertook one more trip into the local region. "You can't go without seeing our Wenchi Crater," Andy, our tour guide, insisted, and he was right. From an altitude of 9,800 feet, we were astonished to see a gigantic crater lake in the middle of the countryside that looked just like a Swiss lake. It was a pity that we did not have much time for such a breathtaking experience. So we had to put off the young lads with their horses that had been saddled and prepared for a trek until a possible later visit.

The Wenchi Crater Lake near Waliso.

Haile – the first meeting

On the journey back I could no longer repress my anxiety. Is he there or not? We were delighted by the surprisingly green and not, as many had expected, arid landscape, but the purpose of our trip was to meet the man who was known locally as "hero" or even "Emperor". I therefore kept my eye on Amanuel as he repeatedly dialed Haile's number on his cell phone. Later, Haile told me what he did to protect himself from the endless phone calls. He only answered calls from his most important friends and contacts. Amanuel was, at that time, not one of those VIPs.

Finally, in his desire to help his first running tour group, he had a bright idea. He suddenly thought of his uncle, who was a national team coach. Dr. Yilma Berta. He answered the phone. "Doctor," Amanuel always called his uncle by his title, "can you help us? Haile knows that we are here, but is he there, and if so, where?" The "Doctor" promised to do his best.

For me the distance grew longer and longer, the questions of my impatient traveling companions more and more intrusive, one Editor in Chief already saw his next, already advertised front page falling through. Then, the awaited solution, which came in the suburbs of Addis Ababa. Haile was not only there, he was waiting for us in the Alem Building, or more precisely, in a club room of his new high-rise cinema. This news triggered excitement and enthusiastic cheering in the bus.

Haile receives this specially made Abebe Bikila t-shirt.

How does one go about meeting a hero? With respect and due deference? These kinds of questions were immediately superfluous. Haile was suddenly standing amongst us in a red Adidas tracksuit and shook all of our hands. "Welcome, how are you?", he said and offered us a seat and something to drink. "I am very pleased that you have come despite our difficult situation at the moment. It is really something special." And then he added: "Until now, it was always us Ethiopians who went to Germany. Now, at last you have come to see us. Congratulations. Please come back again and again!" He sat down on the armrest of one of the club chairs and looked at our group. Even though

> ***Addis Ababa:** at an altitude of between 5,900 and 8,200 feet, Addis Ababa ("new flower") is the highest city in Africa and the third highest in the world. It was first crowned the capital at the end of the 19th Century by Emperor Menelik. The average temperature is 61°F. The number of inhabitants is rising daily and has been estimated at 5 million. The city is full of contrasts: tower blocks, wide, tree-lined streets, enormous markets, beautiful villas, good hotels, but also a large number of corrugated iron huts and traditional stone houses.*

it separated immediately, because everyone immediately wanted to get autographs on letters, photos, t-shirts and elsewhere (who knew how much time Haile had?), he was able to get a look at his out of the ordinary visitors. They already seemed a little unusual to him. There was Sigrid, who had completed 1000 Marathons, Asta, who walked all the long distances, Elke, who had trekked through Ethiopia as a student before Haile was even born, Gerd and Liesel, who organized innovative races, Dieter-Max, who "collected" Marathon races in capital cities of the world. Wolfgang, who organized a reservoir race in Vogtland. He seemed to be particularly taken with the 'thousand Marathon runner', and asked repeatedly if he had understood the figure correctly. (Years later he still asked me if this lady was still around…) Then he laughed again his unmistakable, hearty laugh and apologized for not being able to manage such a figure, but he would run his whole life long, "as long as my legs will carry me." For: "running is life, also my life."

He had just been in London. At the Marathon, with which he had a contractual obligation, he was only able to fire the starting pistol due to a recurring Achilles tendon injury. However, it was not far away from where he was awarded a special honor. He, a non-academic, was awarded an honorary doctorate of law by Dublin University, acknowledging Haile's services to social reform projects and his global running successes. The fact was mentioned that despite his acquired wealth he stayed in his own country. Haile with his dry humor on the last fact: "They couldn't know how comfortable my country is. For me, Ethiopia is the most comfortable country in the world."

This period, in which we were the first German running group to visit him in his African highlands, was one of change for Haile. After his Olympic victories in Atlanta and Sydney, and his fifth place in Athens, he swapped mentally and physically from the 10km on the track to the 42.195km Marathon distance. After a very successful attempt three years earlier in Great Britain, he was now preparing himself for the fast Amsterdam course. Of course, the questions of world records and victories on the longest of all classical race distances were unavoidable. Here the only 5'5" tall man with the typically thick black hair and the ever-present charming smile proved once more to be

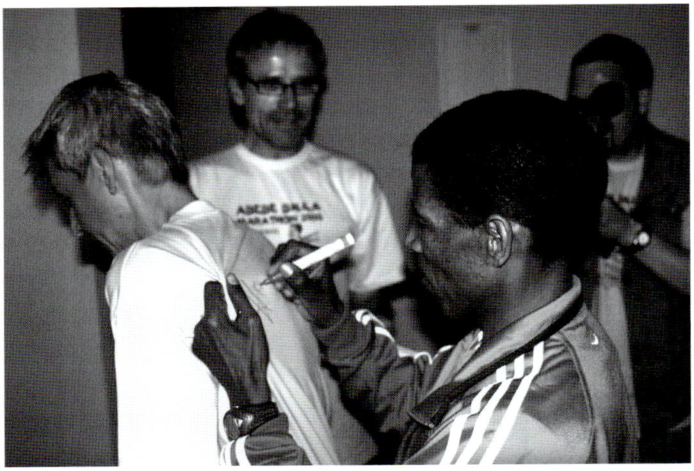

The first German running group at Haile's house.

a master tactician. He never predicted records in advance; he just wanted to win. And legendary compatriot Abebe Bikila, in whose memorial race his German guests were to take part, was present in his thoughts and plans.

On the way to a joint souvenir photo, Haile arranged two surprises. The first, an unexpected invitation received with cheering: "When you come back from your trip to the south, I would like to entertain you at my house." The second was a question, connected with many good wishes for the coming Marathon: "Do you know that the Abebe Bikila Marathon was the first competition in my life?

Haile's first running adventure

Really, he only remembers when he is asked explicitly. Actually, then at the age of sixteen, he didn't want to run a Marathon at all. But he did know from the Olympic radio reports the length of this race, but had never covered anywhere near this distance in the Oromo region where he lived. He had traveled from Asela, his home town, in the overland bus to Addis Ababa, because his older brothers who lived there and ran for the police club, encouraged him to run in a 15km race. Haile saved up the 15 Birr (about $1.5) for a ticket, a quantity of coins that he had never held in his hand before. His father was angry at his son's plans, which he called "silly" and an "unnecessary waste of time." There were many such confrontations between father and son, who absolutely wanted to become a runner. "Become a lawyer, teacher or carpenter, Haile" the settled farmer and owner of vast fields of wheat and corn told him again and again, "if you don't want to take over looking after our land." It was just that now that his third-oldest son was sixteen, in Ethiopian eyes he was now allowed to make his own choices.

Haile swayed in the rickety bus, which barely stuck to a timetable, for hours in the middle of tightly packed sitting and standing men and women to Addis Ababa. For the first time, he set eyes on the vastness of the capital city, whose millions were estimated at between 4 and 5 and at an average of 7,875 feet the highest altitude city in Africa. "I was pulled all over the place," Haile still recounts today. "On the one hand, I felt overpowered by the old, splendid monuments, also the first tower blocks and the unfamiliar traffic, but on the other hand, I was shocked by the beggars, cripples and the squalid huts." Where he came from there was no electricity or running water, but there were no begging children either. It was a good that Tekeye collected him from the bus station and took him to his house. I would never have coped on my own." But Tekeye had to give his brother bad news. The 15km race had been canceled at short notice without reason. Haile was very angry.

June 19th 1988, Haile Gebrselassie at 16 years of age ran in Addis Ababa in the 4th Abebe Bikila Marathon in 2:48 with no special preparation and finished in 99th place. That was his first official competition and he still had no affiliation to a club.

To try to cheer him up, Tekeye told him that on the Sunday, a Marathon would be taking place in honor of the double Olympic champion Abebe Bikila, already in its fourth year, starting in the Central Stadium. "Perhaps you could just give it a try!"

An oil painting of one of his first races.

We were told that the young Gebrselassie wanted to see the course the day before the Marathon and while doing so got hopelessly lost in a really confusing network of streets as though he was in a maze. Nobody knew the name of the street in which his brother lived. Finally he looked for somewhere to sleep on the edge of a street, walked on the morning of the race totally the worse for wear to the stadium, the only one in the city, where he was greeted with relief by his brother who had naturally been worried and blamed himself. Then came the start for several hundred men and women, including Haile. "I didn't know what I had let myself in for. I should have left it. Until the 20km mark, it was going really well though the many streets, across squares, on sidewalks and even down steps. The many cheering and clapping people on the sidelines were unfamiliar to me but they spurred me on. I probably ran too fast."

Round huts in Asela, where Haile grew up.

"In any case I needed all my energy to keep going. I fell over the finish line and found out later that I was 99th. Tekeye, who climbed onto the podium for finishing second and received an envelope containing a small amount of money, brought his little brother who could barely manage by himself with swollen feet, back to the bus that would take him home to Asela. "I was completely shattered after this Marathon. I was aching for a week and lay in bed all day and couldn't work. Never again!"

The man who won Gold barefoot

Sixteen years after this debut by Haile Gebrselassie, nearly two dozen casual runners were now about to run the 21st Abebe Bikila Marathon. But before mixing it with the Ethiopian elite, they went in search of the grave of the founding father, the founder of all African running history, that of Abebe Bikila. The last resting place of the two-time Olympic champion was in the cemetery of St Joseph's Church in Addis Ababa. We found it easily, although the by wrought iron fences surrounded family graves were crammed together.

Abebe Bikila can already be seen from far off, he seems to be waving, but on closer inspection, it is obvious that the stonemason has hewn the eternal monument of the wiry runner at the moment of victory in Rome. Around it were thick chains that were decorated with the Olympic rings. We climbed over them carefully and laid a green wreath. On its bow was written this sentence: "In memory of the Marathon legend Abebe Bikila". Numerous cemetery visitors noticed the unusual group of white men and women who were all paying their respects wearing yellow t-shirts on which the image of that unforgettable Ethiopian was clearly visible.

Abebe Bikila:
born on August 7th 1932 in Jato, died October 25th 1973 in Addis Ababa. First African Olympic champion. Gold in the 1960 Rome Olympic Games (2:15:16) and in Tokyo in 1964 (2:12:11). A knee injury forced him to miss the Mexico City Olympics in 1968. He competed in 26 Marathons. Best time over 10km: 29:00.8 (1962 in Berlin). A car accident in the autumn of 1968 made him paraplegic, but he still took part in toboggan races in Norway and in the Paralympics in archery.

The story of Abebe Bikila is the stuff of legend. He grew up in a time where the Italians were trying to conquer the then Abyssinia. Still today, the Ethiopians are proud that no power has ever been able to colonize their African homeland. Abebe lived in the Oromo region, from where later a myriad of famous running stars would originate. To start with, his daily life was not that different from that of other village children: looking after cattle and goats, threshing corn, carrying water. Later, going to a church school enabled him to do what made him stand out from his peers, he learned to read and write. After that he became a soldier and then even a bodyguard of Emperor Haile Selassie once he returned from exile after the Italian invaders had been driven out; it must have been a real adventure. As a sixteen year-old, he had to march with a letter of

Abebe Bikila became the first ever black African Olympic Champion in Rome in 1960.

recommendation right across Ethiopia to join the Imperial Guard. There he was accepted, and he soon enjoyed many privileges such as watching films in the Emperor's cinema. When he saw on those flickering strips the first Ethiopian Olympic team marching into the Melbourne stadium in 1956, he was so inspired that he started training and entered the Army championships. There he was spotted by Onni Niskanen, a Swedish coach who was born in Finland and who since 1947 had been working on developing Ethiopian athletics. He went up with his Protégés already from the 7,874 feet altitude Addis Ababa to the 2,000 feet higher Entoto Hills in order to take advantage of the more oxygen-rich blood. In this way he combined track training in the only stadium with cross-country runs of up to 15 or 20 miles.

The preparation for the Rome summer Olympics seems almost unbelievable in retrospect. Abebe Bikila ran 20 miles twice in the week before his first ever Marathon, which he finished in a surprising 2:21:23 (at Addis Ababa altitude!), and only one month later turned up at the Olympic Games in the "eternal city". There he was a complete unknown, one of the few participants competing under the green-yellow and red flat of Ethiopia, then still with Selassie's lion in the center. The lean man stood out because of his deep brown skin, but mainly for a strange reason: he was not wearing any shoes. Abebe had owned a pair, but they had not withstood the training in Rome. He therefore decided he would rather run barefoot than take the risk of running in brand-new shoes. He also felt more confident running barefoot as he had already run that first Marathon without shoes.

Abebe Bikila and Mamo Wolde are buried in the cemetery of the St Joseph's church in Addis Ababa.

In burning hot temperatures, even at 6 o'clock in the evening, the 69 competitors set off on the 26 mile, 385 yard course. Even so the starting pace was grueling. The highly favored favorites held back, the Moroccan Rhadi Ben Abdesselem and Abebe Bikila did not. From 20km they had shaken off all their rivals, at 41km in the spotlight of the escort vehicle of the Ethiopian his Moroccan companion had no chance with a quick burst of speed. 2:15:16,2 – a world record! The reporters were speechless. Nobody knew the barefoot runner from Africa and any interviews he gave were difficult as he spoke Amharic. The irony was obvious – in the Olympic year 1936, Italians tried to conquer Ethiopia and 24 years later, an Ethiopian conquered Rome…

Four years after Rome, Abebe, now in the best running shoes and white socks, had the perfect triumph, that only the German Waldemar Cierpinski could emulate. He became Olympic Champion for the second time in Tokyo despite undergoing surgery on his appendix three weeks before. Barely anyone had believed in a gold medal there. And the unchallenged manner of his victory, again in record time! The Marathon victory seemed, as could be seen then on the television images, not even to have taken all his strength. Right after crossing the finish line, he lay down on the grass, not to rest but to give a thorough demonstration of his habitual gymnastic exercises.

The tragedies of two triumphators

In Olympic Mexico in 1968, Abebe Bikila tried it again. However, now a corporal in the Imperial Guard, he went to the Marathon start with shin splints, without thinking he had much of a chance. The day before, he had said to his countryman Mamo Wolde: “You know I’m not going to win, but you can and must. I will support you over the first miles.” Wolde was an experienced Olympian. He had already been on the first Ethiopian Olympic team in 1956, then as a middle-distance runner, not emerging from the pack. But now, 12 years later, the running world looked very different. Over 10km he had already won a silver medal and was eager to try the longest running distance. For 15km, Abebe Bikila managed to keep up his third Olympic challenge, then he gave up. Mamo Wolde though was the unchallenged champion of Mexico City. The spectacular Ethiopian Marathon winning streak thus remained unbroken.

Five months later a traffic accident occurred below the Entoto Hills on the training route to Sheno. All attempts to reconstruct it have until now been unsuccessful. Nobody, not even Haile Gebrselassie, knows whether the hero of Rome and Tokyo was struck by a car or he himself drove into another car. He himself never talked in detail about it; perhaps he couldn’t, or didn’t want to. Now the tragedy would take its course. Having narrowly escaped death, despite operations and nine-months therapy, paraplegia confined him to a wheelchair. He died at the age of 41 in 1973, after being made guest of honor at the Munich Olympics in 1972 and finishing ninth in the Paralympics archery competition. He is survived by four children.

Mamo Wolde

The grave of Abebe Bikila on which German Marathon runners laid a wreath.

Mamo Wolde still played an Olympic role for a few more years. Emperor Haile Selassie received the newly-crowned Olympic Champion from Mexico, who was also part of his Imperial Guard, and promoted him to Captain. It is not know whether he welcomed him in the same way as he had done Abebe Bikila, with his favorite lion from his private zoo as a special tribute. In Munich, although the American Frank Shorter broke the Ethiopian winning streak, the now 40 year-old Mamo Wolde did manage to get among the marathon medalists once again by winning bronze.

Afterwards, he became more and more involved in the intrigues of three political systems. The Emperor was dethroned, the Imperial Guard sent home, but the new man, Colonel Mengistu Haile Mariam, was very quick to remember the sports stars of the east African highlands. The oft-decorated Olympian Wolde did not escape from the lucrative offer to work in the ranks of the Revolutionary Government. Even in uniform. There he became involved in a confrontation with rebellious youths in which a sixteen year-old was killed after an exchange of shots. Exactly what happened in that bar in Addis Ababa has never really been explained. As at the start of the 1990s Mengistu was banished and an interim government under Meles Zenawi took over, the Olympic champion was severely criticized over that incident and imprisoned in 1993. Not till 9 years later, he received a legal notification informing him of a six-year jail term, and was released. Mamo Wolde died that same year of liver cancer, a broken man whose family suffered greatly from this tragic end.

Mamo Wolde:
born on June 12th 1932 in Diri Jille, died on May 26th 2002 in Addis Ababa. He competed in four Olympic Games: 1956 Melbourne: 800m, 1500m, 4 x 400m (no medals), 1964 Tokyo: fourth over 10K (28:31.8), moved up to the Marathon 1968 in Mexico: Gold Marathon (2:20:26.4), Silver 10K (29:28.0), 1972 Munich: Bronze Marathon (2:15:08).

As we walked away from the Abebe Bikila memorial in the central cemetery, a knowledgeable guide of our running tour group pointed out a nearby plot, which was that of Mamo Wolde. He had himself competed in the Olympic Marathon of Mexico City and finished a respectable 17th: Manfred Steffny. Mamo's place of rest seemed less conspicuous and less well tended. "Perhaps we should have also honored him in his last resting place with a wreath?"

The Abebe Bikila Marathon – an extraordinary experience

The Marathon in honor of the founding father of all Ethiopian runners already established a tradition. In the year of our visit, the number 21 appeared on the starting banner. It was a chance for successors to Haile, Tulu & Co. to be spotted, in the company of some foreign guests, e.g. from neighboring Kenya and Urundi, for example. Actually, we casual runners from central Europe were just a sideshow, but as our appearance was unprecedented at the Abebe Bikila Marathon before, we were an exotic one. Head Coach Dr. Woldemeskel Kostre, with the famous walking aid, greeted us just as warmly as other coaches who had fond memories of studying in Leipzig or Cologne. Only the General Secretary asked gently how much extra time his timekeepers would really be needed for. Already in the preparation for this our debut, we had, not least because of the unfamiliar altitude of over 7,874 feet, asked the organizing Ethiopian Athletics Federation to time us over half Marathon and 10km as well, which was something new for them and could only be achieved after much negotiation from our friend Amanuel.

The start was delayed. Not because of the African sense of time, but due to the fact that the "new flower" Addis Ababa on that Sunday had not yet flowered. Strikes were still casting its shadow over the capital, so no bus drivers and only a few taxi drivers turned their engines on, which meant that few runners made it from the suburbs to the central stadium. The organizers sent off the first group with a good 30-minutes start, the second with almost an hour delay into the city center. With the approximately 150 women, all small, slender girls in their mid 20s, could the seniors start running "from 45", it was noted.

HAILE GEBRSELASSIE

21st Abebe Bikila Marathon, June 12 2005, Addis Ababa, approx. 150 women (women and seniors (+45) and 450 men from African countries, and for the first time 15 German runners. 6,500 to 7,500 feet altitude, 77°F.

Winners: Josef Nideti (Kenya) 2:12:22 and Worknesh Tola (Ethiopia) 2:54:08

None of the Ethiopians could have been over 50, which was the age of the youngest of us Germans. The German running tourists were therefore already in Meskel Square, right behind the stadium, at the end of the running line. The few spectators who stood at the edges of the streets after the following day's turbulence had a lot of sympathy for the chasing pack of foreigners, the 'Ferendschis'. To still be fit at such an age is valued by Ethiopians, whose average life-expectancy is in the late forties. However, while the leading group of women was protected by a police vehicle escort, we had to struggle not only with the unfamiliar altitude but also soon against exhaust fumes and a lack of course markings. We all ran through it, onetheless. Past Haile Gebrselassie's tower block and past mud huts, fruit and vegetable markets, even sometimes running around a few donkey carts. The streets, among them the high Ring Road, were in immaculate condition throughout, the climbs made the altitude running even more difficult. Each one of us wondered en route: What would the almost chaotic traffic look like on a strike-free Sunday? Drinks? Bananas? Thanks to the Ethiopian travel agent and its escort vehicles, nothing was lacking. One of us had an extraordinary experience. From one watering station, two young spectators accompanied him running for many miles, carried his plastic bottle and always showed him the correct route in the winding alleys of downtown Gola Sefer.

A runner is greeted by the Ethiopian folklore dancers.

Rapturous applause greeted the half-Marathon runners as they turned with some of the male Ethiopian Marathon runners into the stadium lap. The stands were filling up, which, as it turned out, was largely due to an upcoming soccer match. The soccer fans' greatest applause was for our tail-ender who had walked the 26 miles 385 yards right to the end and marched alone, but waving, down the finishing straight. Although no helper from the organizing team had timed his walked race, our friend Amanuel had got hold of a stopwatch.

More than 300 locals, almost all in running shoes, faced the challenge of running a Marathon and the critical gaze of the top coaches, who stood at the finish and took notes. At about 2 hours, 50 minutes they put their stopwatches away. That was enough for them; they had timed about 100 men. The fastest of them were honored with the fanfare of trumpets and money. But which of them would run in Haile's footsteps? The acknowledgement of the German athletes, whose participation was a kind of first in the land of runners, was obvious. All were invited to the closing banquet, which was actually only intended for medallists. The race director gave a nice speech, in which he welcomed future European visitors and announced a special surprise. A green, yellow and red Adidas tracksuit with 'Ethiopia' on the back had been made for each of the runners from Germany. We celebrated our new friends and promised to return.

Every German premier runner in the Abebe Bikila Marathon congratulated himself for having completed the course at this altitude. The victory ceremonies of the Africans were already over by this time.

That Sunday evening, Haile telephoned our hotel and asked if we were feeling the after-effects of our Marathon. "See you Thursday evening then," he said when we told him we were happy. "I'm happy to meet you again. Welcome!"

The trip to the green south

Haile Gebrselassie raved about the south of the Ethiopian highlands. In Hawassa, his first four star hotel was being built, right in the famous Great Rift Valley, whose 3,700 miles also run through Ethiopia. Amanuel had already included this breathtaking landscape in our travel itinerary. And so we chugged along in the mini bus to Lake Langano, one of the many lakes near the national park. The 170 mile trip there seemed almost double the length on the partly unsurfaced roads, but was scattered with sights of interest. And so we admired for the first time a rock church in Aladi Maryam, “A small one”, as leader Andy emphasized, and immediately commented that we absolutely had to visit Lalibela in the north, where a dozen or more similar ones had been arranged in a kind of chain. These churches are like symbols of the long Christian history of the Ethiopian people, sanctuaries hewn out of the rocky ground over 700 years ago. Still today, the Christian Orthodox religion prevails in a nation of 80 million inhabitants with its approximately 80 nationalities, although Islam has almost caught up. From the diverse culture of the past, we were impressed on our journey by 18 foot high pillars and tombs, more brightly colored than any we had ever seen. On them were painted lions, monkeys and thickly-bearded human heads, even weapons.

The inviting Langano Lake, with its bungalow village can only be highly recommended, as can other lodges and basic but clean tourist huts. In southerly Arba Minch, on the highway to Kenya, from the Bekele Mola Hotel we could not get enough of looking at the fascinating views over the low-lying Seen Abaya and Chamo. Through the latter we made a foray on a boat built for tourists. It even had a Roof, and its only fault was that its engine kept on breaking down. But this gave us plenty of time to observe not only pelicans, ospreys and herons in their droves, but also to get really close to a few hippos and crocodiles. Another adventure.

Even more memorable was the visit to that mountain above the “40 springs” (or “Arba Minch“ in Amharic), where the indigenous Dorze people, no longer warlike as they once were, can be found. In humble dwellings also glad to welcome European visitors whom they greeted with acrobatic dancing and by trying to sell them brightly knitted caps or a coffee ceremony. Day after day, the women and girls of the tribe are sent into the valley, into the city, with yard-long bamboo poles tied together by two ropes over the shoulders. Ten miles down with about 66 pounds in weight, and then return with 20 Birr (2 dollars) again to cover the same distance into the high village. And the thing we found hardest to understand: always with a smile on their faces.

An interesting southern road: Addis Ababa, Adadi Maryam (rock churches), Tiya and Silte (field of steles), Langano Lake (safe to swim in), Abyata Shala National Park (ostriches, hot springs), Sasheme (Rastas from Jamaica), Awasa (fish market), Arba Minch (crocodile market, Lake Chamo with hippos, crocodiles), Chencha (center of the Dorze People, folkloric cotton weaving).

The trip back to Addis Ababa brought us close to the green south and the friendly inhabitants of many areas, whether in Sidamo, Bale or Arsi. It was always more interesting off the beaten track. For example in a village whose name I unfortunately did not make a note of, where for a round of coffee, we moved all the plastic chairs in a street café together. The whole village ran there to see the white people from another world and to wave at them enthusiastically. Our yellow t-shirts quickly proved to be the best introduction and admission ticket wherever we went. Although nobody could have deciphered the writing "Abebe Bikila Marathon 2005", everyone knew the hero of Rome and Tokyo. This always prompted two other well understood words: "Haile Gebrselassie". There was shaking of hands and loud cheering. We were now immersed in Haile's world.

On our return journey we repeatatly noticed the many men and women who walked for miles along the country roads. With water canisters and bundles of wood on their backs or driving herds of animals before them. School children carried their books in their hands. Andy told us: "on weekdays they usually run between 6 and 10 miles to class and of course the same distance back home again. Because of this, not many of them are sent to school by their parents but into the fields instead." How can this problem be solved? Andy: "by halving the journeys by building new schools, I think." This led to complex deliberations among our bus group. It had long been understood that sweets in Ethiopia were (still) frowned upon (Andy: "Healthy teeth are really important to us!") Distributing clothing can only be a short-term aid ("As people will expect that will always come with things"). This was how the German Running tourists came up with the idea between Sashemene and Zebre of building a village school in Ethiopia wherever it was particularly needed with donations from Marathon runners. And we wanted to tell this result of our first running trip to Ethiopia to the man who was not only a famous running miracle but who also made miracles happen – Haile Gebrselassie.

HAILE GEBRSELASSIE

At home with Haile

We did not find his house straight away. None of our Ethiopian advisors had ever been fortunate enough to be invited to his house. The direction, east of Addis Ababa, was clear. As we went uphill, we asked for directions. "Haile? Yeah? Up there!" However, all we found was the iron gate of the rear entrance that we knocked on loudly to draw attention to ourselves. By the time the gatekeeper had noticed us, Haile was already there, this time in a light gray three-striped tracksuit, laughing at our entrance to his home. "My guests normally use the front entrance," and added: "You really are something special." He insisted on shaking hands with and welcoming each and every one of us. Usually the Ethiopian way, where the left hand holds one's own right hand, a custom that we were told dates from former more warlike times when the greeter did this to show that he was not carrying weapons. Haile himself kindly offered us a choice of drinks: water, wine, beer, even Cola.

The Gebrselassie villa high above the city of Addis Ababa can absolutely be compared to an ambassador's residence. The "runner of the century" makes no secret of the fact that his victories and records have earned him a few millions. He has mainly invested them in social projects, housing and business and has taken his brothers, sisters and father under his wing. There is hardly a single one of the roughly 80 million Ethiopians, many of them among the poorest in the world, who would begrudge him his running riches. Haile has remained one of them. And asked about their hopes concerning his future, they not only mention his World Championships and Olympic titles, but also their wish that they would like to see him elected President of their country. Emperor Haile Gebrselassie.

Haile introduced us to his three daughters and Alem, his wife and business partner. Then he led us through his elegantly decorated room: tasteful antique chairs, leather-covered, cushions with the lion symbol of Haile Selassie, heavy, bright curtains, which nevertheless allowed a fantastic panorama over his home city of Addis Ababa below.

Haile is amazed by a special present: gloves signed by double Olympic champion Waldemar Cierpinski.

Oriental-patterned carpets and an enormous television, which unlike Haile worked around the clock. A spiral staircase led up to the bedrooms and guestrooms. High and wide glass-fronted cabinets contained countless cups, vases, figurines, pictures and medals. One was missing, the Gold medal from Atlanta, his first Olympic victory medal. He had donated it to the Kidame Mirete Church, a pilgrimage site in the Entoto Hills, which was also often the meeting and starting point for elite athletes' training.

Haile Gebrselassie's family live in the eastern suburbs of Addis Ababa and consists (as of 2008) of Haile, his wife Alem (born 04/13/74) and their three daughters Eden (5/18/98), Melat (04/02/2000) and Betty (04/02/2000) and son Naty (09/15/2005).

We went down a couple of steps, where Haile spread out his arms: "I am going to bring all my trophies and presents down here and put them in chronological order." One of the guests interrupted him with an inquisitive, but not uninteresting question: "How long do you think you will go on collecting them?"

To which Haile replied wisely and with his famous laugh: "as long as I can. And you should know that I'll still be running when I'm 66." He said it with a look at some of those standing around him.

In the kitchen, an authentic Ethiopian buffet had been prepared for us. For foreigners, the cuisine in this ancient African country may be something of an acquired taste, but we were used to it, having just completed a journey of discovery through part of Ethiopia. So we rightly shunned the use of knives and forks, in order to enjoy the spicy pieces of braising steak ("Wot") in different sauces. For this we used the "Injera", a cake-like flat bread made of local grain ("Teff"), but also containing milo and barley. "Good for runners," says Haile, and Eden, the oldest daughter, added: "And makes you strong." At which she tried to flex her biceps. The soft, flat cakes tasted sour and were torn into mouth-size pieces, which were wrapped around the pieces of meat and then pushed into our mouths. Often for an evening party, a large, brightly-colored basket ("Mesob") was served, on which the host laid enormous flat Injera cakes. The hands are washed before and after eating. It is also customary for the host to place a particularly appetizing morsel in a guest's mouth as a sign of respect or friendship ("Gursha"). Haile omitted this on this occasion, probably due to our numbers.

Instead there were discussions that centered on running and life in Ethiopia. We described how hard it was for European casual runners to participate in a very high-quality Abebe Bikila Marathon and encouraged the extension of the 'Great Ethiopian Run', for which Haile had taken over sponsorship.

Food is laid out on a large plate or basket table and traditionally eaten without cutlery with a soft flat bread, meat and many spicy sauces. On fast days (Wednesdays and Fridays), no meat is eaten. Coffee to finish is a must. Before and after eating, the hands are washed, usually in passed around bowls.

A 10km race, which fortunately in Addis Ababa every year at the end of November brought thousands onto the Bole Road, was understandably not enough to motivate any Europeans to fly to the middle of Africa. Perhaps the land of the runners should organize its own 'Ethiopia Marathon', also with shorter distances?

Such ideas naturally remained in Haile's house at first. Not so though the proposal that had been born on the way back from the south and which was also relayed to the host; a school for Ethiopia. Haile was surprised and immediately taken by our idea. He himself suggested a name for the future project, which should be built somewhere in the highlands: "Call the school "Marathon", for it is you who want to build it."

When it was time to say goodbye because of our flight back to Germany, we all met again on the terrace of Haile's house. Down below twinkled the lights of the lively, million-strong city of Addis Ababa. In all the excitement, and in this special atmosphere, we nearly forgot to give the 10km double Olympic champion a special souvenir – a pair of thin running gloves signed by the double Olympic Marathon champion Waldemar Cierpincki.

Guests in Haile's house.

Haile laughed again in his charming way and commented quick-wittedly: "I suppose you have realized that it is cold 9,800 feet up in the hills. I will make good use of them." What he thought about the suggestion that he was the successor of Cierpinski or Abebe Bikila, he did not want to let on at the time.

Dehna hun (good bye), Haile. You, and Ethiopia, will see us again!

"Marathon" – A School for Ethiopia

Dear Friends and Partners,

for the first time, a group of German runners took part in the Abebe Bikila Marathon in Addis Ababa, which brought great recognition from the Ethiopian partners and hosts. After seeing the everyday living problems of the people during an excursion through the country, the group decided to support their Ethiopian friends with a concrete project. They suggested raising money in Germany to have a new school built with the symbolic name 'Marathon'.

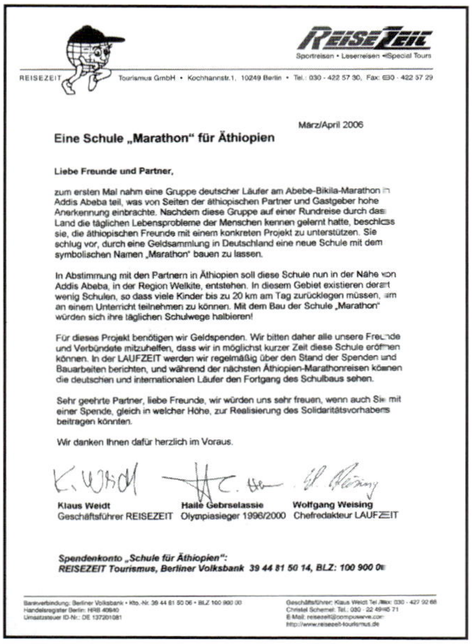

REISEZEIT Sportreisen • Leserreisen • Special Tours

REISEZEIT Tourismus GmbH • Kochhannstr.1, 10249 Berlin • Tel.: 030 - 422 57 30, Fax: 030 - 422 57 29

März/April 2006

Eine Schule „Marathon" für Äthiopien

Liebe Freunde und Partner,

zum ersten Mal nahm eine Gruppe deutscher Läufer am Abebe-Bikila-Marathon in Addis Abeba teil, was von Seiten der äthiopischen Partner und Gastgeber hohe Anerkennung einbrachte. Nachdem diese Gruppe auf einer Rundreise durch das Land die täglichen Lebensprobleme der Menschen kennen gelernt hatte, beschloss sie, die äthiopischen Freunde mit einem konkreten Projekt zu unterstützen. Sie schlug vor, durch eine Geldsammlung in Deutschland eine neue Schule mit dem symbolischen Namen „Marathon" bauen zu lassen.

In Abstimmung mit den Partnern in Äthiopien soll diese Schule nun in der Nähe von Addis Abeba, in der Region Welkite, entstehen. In diesem Gebiet existieren derart wenig Schulen, so dass viele Kinder bis zu 20 km am Tag zurücklegen müssen, um an einem Unterricht teilnehmen zu können. Mit dem Bau der Schule „Marathon" würden sich ihre täglichen Schulwege halbieren!

Für dieses Projekt benötigen wir Geldspenden. Wir bitten daher alle unsere Freunde und Verbündete mitzuhelfen, dass wir in möglichst kurzer Zeit diese Schule eröffnen können. In der LAUFZEIT werden wir regelmäßig über den Stand der Spenden und Bauarbeiten berichten, und während der nächsten Äthiopien-Marathonreisen können die deutschen und internationalen Läufer den Fortgang des Schulbaus sehen.

Sehr geehrte Partner, liebe Freunde, wir würden uns sehr freuen, wenn auch Sie mit einer Spende, gleich in welcher Höhe, zur Realisierung des Solidaritätsvorhabens beitragen könnten.

Wir danken Ihnen dafür herzlich im Voraus.

Klaus Weidt	Haile Gebrselassie	Wolfgang Weising
Geschäftsführer REISEZEIT	Olympiasieger 1996/2000	Chefredakteur LAUFZEIT

Spendenkonto „Schule für Äthiopien":
REISEZEIT Tourismus, Berliner Volksbank 39 44 81 50 14, BLZ: 100 900 00

Bankverbindung: Berliner Volksbank • Kto.-Nr. 39 44 81 50 06 • BLZ 100 900 00
Handelsregister Berlin: HRB 40940
Umsatzsteuer ID-Nr.: DE 137201081

Geschäftsführer: Klaus Weidt Tel./Fax: 030 - 427 92 68
Christel Schemel: Tel.: 030 - 22 49 85 71
E-Mail: reisezeit@compuserve.com
http://www.reisezeit-tourismus.de

In agreement with the partners in Ethiopia, this school should be built near Addis Ababa, in the region of Welkite. There are few schools of this kind in this area, so that many children have to travel up to 15 miles a day to be able to attend class. Building the 'Marathon' school will halve their daily journey to school!

For this project, we need money. We therefore ask all our friends and allies, so we can open this school as quickly as possible. During the construction process, we shall report regularly on the status of donations and building work, and during the next Ethiopia Marathon trip, the German and International runners can see how the school building is progressing.

Esteemed partners, dear friends, we would be delighted if you could also make a donation, no matter how much, to help make this joint venture become reality.

Thank you very much in advance

Klaus Weidt	*Haile Gebrselassie*
Wolfgang Weising	
ReiseZeit MD	*Olympic Champion 1996/2000*
Editor in Chief Laufzeit	

2 From the Arsi Highlands to the World of Running

The man who discovered the running prodigy

One man stayed in the background in the Gebrselassie's house although his impressive stature and groomed appearance made him difficult to ignore. At some point Haile had introduced him and some of us even spoke with him, as he spoke good English. However, he always kept himself in the background. He was the "doctor", Amanuel's uncle, the man as I first learned in a subsequent visit, who had discovered the talented Haile in the rural Arsi Province. A unique find in a fertile countryside, as it turned out.

Haile with coach Dr. Yilma Berta.

Dr. Yilma Berta, a middle-distance runner from Debre Zeit, the renamed Bishoftu in the Oromo Province, had once accepted a lucrative offer from Prague and studied there at one of the oldest Universities in Europe. For eight years he lived in the "Golden City" in Moldavia, where he successfully completed two doctoral theses on Training Methods and Training Forms for Students. With two children, he returned home at the start of the 1980s and found work at the Committee for Sport, where he was not only coach for distances between 800m and 10K, but also for youth talent spotting.

Ethiopian Airlines, Africa's largest airline, had at that time, provided funding for the development of running talent, not least in the furor after the Gold medal won in Moscow. They offered to sponsor the successors to Miruts

Yifter and collaborated with the Athletics Federation on a "Marathon Pilot Project". The tall, dark "doctor" took it to the Arsi Province, south east of Addis Ababa, where the majority of Oromos live. The surrounding mountains are the ancestral home of this tribe. Many of the Christian Oromos had served in the Imperial Guard of Emperor Haile Selassie, including the running legend Abebe Bikila. In the highlands around Asela, no great skill was required to spot running-crazy farming children. They all had no choice but to run every day: to school, to the watering place, to the animal market, with the herds in the pastures. For the first race, he looked for fifteen, which included a small fellow called Haile Gebrselassie. "He was good, but he didn't win," recalls Yilma Berta, who took some of the best, without him, to the capital city. "Keep on running, I told Haile, and I gave him some tips. I'll be back."

Two years went by, and the coach was curious to see which of the non-selected kids would still show up for a new selection race. It was almost unbelievable; all of them had continued practicing and showed up expectantly. Haile was among them. This time, he let nobody push him out of first place and took gratefully with both hands, as was the Ethiopian custom, the first running shoes and tracksuit he had been given in his life. A prize that the Olympic champion still remembers with fondness today.

When a second race was held later, he won again. Dr. Yilma Berta was looking for 3 running talents, spotted him and invited him to Addis Ababa. "From now on you can train in the Police sports club. Sort it out with your parents, I will wait for you at the stadium."

Arsi Province, with its capital city Asela, lies south east of Addis Ababa. The predominant ethnic group is the Arsi Oromo. The Oromo tribe consists of 200 groups. Its language, Orominya, is spoken in Africa by an estimated 20 million people. Most of Ethiopia's running talent comes from this region.

This brought Haile into conflict with his father, again. For him, running was a waste of time; he could never imagine that one could earn one's living from it and even later support a family. "That is not a good idea, son," he tried to dissuade him. "Learn something useful, like your sisters. If you don't want to plough the fields, then do something else sensible. Please think about it Haile."

The son, now 16 years old, already had given it a lot of thought and would not change his mind. Even after his, naturally unbeknownst to his father, Abebe Bikila Marathon run, which had nearly finished him off, he could not be persuaded to turn down the coach-doctor's offer. Haile traveled resolutely to Addis Ababa and looked in the back streets of the dizzying big city for the small stone house of his big brother.

HAILE GEBRSELASSIE

Haile's childhood – running, running, running

Haile Gebrselassie was born on April 18th, 1973 in Asela, 110 miles south of Addis Ababa. On his Ethiopian ID card, the year is given as 1980, which is confusing for us and should be explained right away. In Gebrselassie's kingdom, the Julian calendar has never been adopted, that calendar according to which year one began only seven years and eight months after the birth of Christ. Even the clocks move differently here, i.e. the day starts at dawn rather than at midnight. Ethiopia is the only country in the world that still measures time in this way but also does not want to change this feature because it is unique.

From the film "Endurance".

Haile was the seventh child of ten of a first marriage. The family was not one of the poor ones of this district; they possessed a parcel of land the grandfather bequeathed them. He must have been a colorful character, a priest who married nine times but only had four children to show for it. Haile's father was the eldest and therefore the main heir. "My father was strong, very strong," explains Haile "often he was, I know one shouldn't say this about a father, unfair. He beat us almost daily, sometimes several times a day. We had to work hard, in the field, on the pastures, in the stables. Twelve hours a day and more. That was normal and even us kids found it quite normal." However, he spoke lovingly about his mother, who, overwhelmed by the work in the house and on the farm, died much

too young of exhaustion. He sensed how much she cared about him, asked about his thoughts and he gladly did as she wished when she asked him in the evenings to read aloud stories from the Bible.

Haile Gebrselassie:
born on April 18th 1973 in Asela. Residence until the age of 16 in a farming village near Asela. His father, Gebrselassie Bekele, was a landowner and cattle farmer. He had 13 children from 2 marriages. Haile's mother died young.

For a long time, all twelve of them lived in the customary Tukul; a round hut with walls of mud, a central pillar, a low door, a straw roof and walls with no windows. Right in the center an open hearth, whose smoke at least kept the insects at bay, a wooden table, stools and mud benches covered in animal skins that were also used for sleeping. The rear of the hut was screened off; here the most valuable domestic animals spent the night. The small town of Asela and of course all surrounding villages already always belonged to the region of the Arsi Oromo, one of Six of the proud tribes with their tall, good-looking peoples. Even today, the man still wear white togas and the women often leather clothing embroidered with pearls.

"When I look back on my childhood," says Haile, "it consisted of hard work and constant running. We had no tractors or other farm machinery." Everything was done by hand, from milking to threshing the grain. Running was quite normal, and it was always at an altitude of at least 6,500 feet. Three miles to the watering place and three miles back with the jugs. Six miles to school and of course, the same distance back. For ten long years. Back on the farm, there were cattle or sheep to chase, to round up and drive back to the village. "This was accidental endurance training, said Haile with a grin, but also a bit like interval training, as it would be called today."

He was seven when a radio report was to have a lasting influence on his life. He only learnt that Ethiopian athletes were taking part in the Moscow Olympic Games from the evening news, for which his father put batteries in the radio, only to remove them again afterwards to save money. Haile noted the time of the radio broadcast of the 10K, took the batteries out of a torch and crept out with the rickety portable radio into the silvery-green cornfield. There he almost jumped and shouted for joy; Miruts Yifter, whom he knew and admired like everyone else, had just followed his bronze medal in Munich, Germany, with Olympic gold. It must have been an exciting race, in which in the last lap Miruts was still boxed in. But then the second Ethiopian Mohammed Kedir created a space for him 300m before the finish line so that he could take the lead. He won Gold medal by 1.6 seconds. A result that made an impression on farm boy Haile, and which actually would never leave him. To emulate Yifter, soon also called "the Shifter".

Haile grew up in a round hut like these "Tukuls". This is also where he learned of Miruts Yifter's Olympic victory (# 191).

In Moscow, Haile explained later, the reporters were confused because in the press conference for Miruts Yifter, two birth years were given, one corresponding to the Ethiopian calendar. When he was asked about his real age, Yifter the Shifter avoided the question by answering: "A man can steal my chickens or my sheep, but nobody can take my age away from me." Then he was silent.

Haile now ran more and more. "My brothers and sisters gradually took over my work so that I could run more. On Sundays I usually ran into the village or into the city to measure myself against other boys. That was exciting and also a nice change."

Miruts Yifter (in Amharic: Muruse Yefter). Born in 1944 in Adrigat, Tigray Province. Worked as a lorry driver and served as a soldier in the Ethiopian Air Force. In the 1972 Olympic Games he finished third in the 10K (he did not start the 5000m final), 1980 Olympic Champion over 10K (27:42.7) and 5K (13:12.0). He has a second home in Canada.

He is grateful to his Physical Education teacher, who advised him to train over plenty of long distances at altitude in Arsi, cross-country and up and down hills. "He thought that I had the makings of a good athlete. That may be an exaggeration but I believed him. I saw how easily I beat all my friends. My oldest brother, who already trained in Addis, also encouraged me."

He was often lost in his own thoughts, which he shared with nobody. So, when he saw airplanes – how do you actually become a pilot? Or an artist? Or a carpenter? Why do monkeys jump so far? How do you get better than other people? And he was convinced that there must be a way to escape from an apparently pre-determined life, to be something other than a farmer. Why not an athlete, a runner like Miruts Yifter?

Father Gebrselassie Bekele just shook his head uncomprehendingly. "You're going to come to no good, son."

With 'energy' to Addis Ababa

Ethiopian names always have a special meaning, just those of many nationalities. One's first name is one's own, the second is the father's; there are no surnames. They usually have a religious origin. Haile means 'power' or 'energy' and Gebrselassie (also written separately Gebr Selassie) means the 'Trinity'.

This energy enabled Haile to become successful more quickly than he could ever have imagined.

View of Addis Ababa.

Dr. Woldemeskel Kostre:
Assistant Coach at the 1972 Olympic Games in Munich. Then national Ethiopian long distance coach from 1980. Studied sports in Budapest in the 1960s and 70s, where he also wrote his doctorate. Under his direction, the Ethiopian Olympic successes of Barcelona in 1992 were achieved. Distinguished by the IAAF, among others.

Dr. Yilma Berta, the sponsor, also oversaw the move of the new talent from Asela to the capital city. To begin with he lived with his elder brother. In answer to Haile's question to the coach whether he would now like to be a Marathon runner, the latter brushed it decisively aside. "Much too soon, you are still too young for that. You would finish well down the field. You should compete over 5K and 10K. First cross-country, then on the track. And he entrusted him to Dr. Woldemeskel Kostre, the strict but successful head coach of the Ethiopian distance running elite. He had come to this post after basic coaching training and a doctorate in Budapest and had held his own in the political turmoil, not least due to the support of the athletes.

Haile trained in different places, in the central stadium of the city, also known as the national stadium or "Addis Ababa Stadium." Of course below the Entoto mountains but also right in the middle of the hilly countryside that unfortunately was becoming more and more deforested. Countless eucalyptus trees were carried down into the valley bundled onto the backs of hundreds of women every day for a couple of Birr, just to survive. However, Haile also ran all over the city, past Meskel Square in Kenyatta Avenue or Churchill Street where it was quite normal for sheep or cattle to wander along the streets despite the chaotic and smelly traffic.

First shy encounter with Alem.

The rookie Gebrselassie was immediately placed next to experienced, leading athletes. Fita Bayisa and Addis Ababa were already stars. Both could demonstrate not only international successes but also considerable prize winnings. "They were actually expecting", reminisced Haile, "that as a young athlete, I would, as is only correct, treat them with respect. Of course I respected them, but not to the extent that I just ran behind them. I could sometimes even be quicker, which annoyed them. I gave everything in every training session and was usually one of the last to stop."

The cross-country terrain of Jan Meda, near the edge of the city, was, as always, included in the training program. This race ground of Addis Ababa, originally belonging to the Emperor, not only provided possibilities for horse-racing but also for 3-4 miles of long cross-country races. This was where the national and international championships were held, and also where, especially on Sundays, the city's running and soccer fanatics met. On the way to Jan Meda, Haile met a girl called Alem. She sold cola and water from her kiosk, where the athletes liked to stop. A friend introduced them to each other, which wreaked havoc with Haile's resting pulse rate. Here too he demonstrated his consistent 'energy': he acquired the telephone number of this drinks kiosk and asked Alem if she would like to meet up with him. The friend, a coach, soon took the two of them to a secluded table in an open air restaurant and left them alone there. Haile ordered cola, Alem tea. There was a long silence, then they began to talk hesitantly. Family here, a strict father there, "did that really Happen to you?" Alem shook her head, explained that she would like to learn to play the piano or to use a computer that she still lived with her parents…The ice was broken.

Haile's first competitions:
3/24/1991: World Junior Cross-Country Championships in Antwerp, Belgium 8420m, 8th place (24:23).
3/21/1992: World Cross-country Championships in Boston, USA, 8000m, 2nd place (23:25).
9/18/1992: World Junior, Championships in Seoul, South Korea, 10K (28:03.99) and 5K (13:36.06) both 1st place.

Via Jan Meda to the Netherlands

Haile has indelible memories of Jan Meda, not only because of Alem, whose name means 'world'. Jan Meda really opened up the world of running to him. Just a few months after being given the membership card for the capital city's police club, the coach sent him to the national cross-country championships. For the young man from the Arsi Highlands, the course in the horse racing track of Jan Meda was no problem. "After all we were just running over the fields at home." He was fifth. He did not give a thought to whether or not he had qualified for the upcoming World Junior Championships. So he was all the more delighted when he was told later that he had been selected and would be flying to Antwerp, Belgium. Haile was already on the national team! A giant leap after such a short time in elite training with the Ethiopian pros.

Manager Jos Hermens (Netherlands) born 1950, several times world record holder, Olympian in Montreal (10K 10th place, Marathon 25th place). Responsible with his son as head of a management agency for athletes from different countries, including Haile Gebrselassie since 1993.

What he did not know then: A Dutch manager, who had had connections with the Ethiopians since the mid-80s, had been watching the cross-country runners in Jan Meda as usual. His name was Jos Hermens. Once himself a top athlete with records and internationally respected performances, had founded Global Sports Communications, a management agency that promoted and represented athletes. He was impressed by 17 year-old Haile's energy and fighting spirit, by a different running style and by the fact that he had only been in Addis Ababa for three months. Hermens spoke to him in English, then in German. Of course he did not speak Amharic, the everyday language in the multiethnic state. A coach helped out a little, but a proper conversation was impossible. But the experienced manager said to himself: "I'm going to keep an eye on him."

He met him again in Antwerp, in the place where in 1991 the title race for the world's best junior cross-country runners was held. For Haile those championships, in which he finished eighth, were less memorable than the journey there. His first time on a plane. "I was nervous and excited, that from so high up you could see everything. I was disappointed that all I could see outside were clouds. I had to go to the toilet. But how did it work in a plane? Did everything fall out? Eventually I asked an air hostess if a window could be opened to get some fresh air. Everyone laughed."

In Brussels, after the landing, the country boy from the Highlands of Arsi-Oromo entered a hotel for the first time. He was amazed by the air conditioning, television sets in all rooms, automatic doors. People did not eat like they did in his country, but with a knife and fork. He was already a little shocked: "the people here must have a lot of money to be able to afford that, I supposed. And I comforted myself with the thought that money is not everything. I have always trusted what God says. One must work hard, like my father, or now I as an athlete, and one must always be there for others. Then God will reward you, then He will give you a fair reward for your hard work."

What he will not forget from Antwerp's 8,420 meters was the Kenyan who finished one place in front of him, Ismail Kirui. He was to remain in his wake for another couple of years.

World Champion – despite a few problems

The year of the Olympic Games in Barcelona fell right in the middle of the political upheaval in the East African nation. Mengistu Haile Mariam had quickly yielded to the attempted coup of a "People's Republic" after the collapse of the Soviet Union and flew to Zimbabwe. The new government was heading for a "Federal Democratic Republic" and declared a "national reorganization". The sports stars were little affected by the turmoil, apart from the issue of future funding.

Despite some of these problems, the Ethiopian runners were extremely successful. Derartu Tulu, also from Haile's Arsi Province, won the Gold medal in the 10K in Barcelona, which made special headlines in the international press: she was the second African woman to be crowned Olympic Champion. Haile's training companions Addis and Fita won Bronze medals. Haile was inspired. After his second cross-country place in Boston, again behind Kirui, with the Olympic images in his head he went to race for the World Junior Championships title in far-off South Korea. This was the scene of his breakthrough. Haile Gebrselassie beat Kirui for the first time over 5000m and secured the Gold medal as he did over twice the distance. Two-time world champion and after only two years' high level training!

Derartu Tulu

The year ended in a similar fashion in Germany, which surely only a few people will remember. In the third Ekiden race from Potsdam to Berlin, $30,000 in prize money was offered, which was this time contested not only by the highly paid Kenyans but also the Ethiopians. The named line-up of that November relay race still makes the mouth water: Olympic bronze medallists Addis Ababa and Fita Bayisa, Worku Bekila, Abraham Assefa and Haile Gebrselassie. Fita Bayisa went off like a rocket, the others took advantage of the lead and Haile (whose name appeared in the newspapers as Haile Selassie), built on it easily like the others. Nobody had a chance against this quintet, the Kenyans, used to winning, just as little as the German relay-runners with Stefan Freigang and Dieter Baumann. That evening, as the Ethiopians opened their envelope full of dollars, Worku asked his friend: "Say, did you see Baumann?

HAILE GEBRSELASSIE

In November 1992, Haile visited Germany for the first time. In the Ekiden race on November 8th, from Potsdam to Berlin, in which the Marathon distance is traditionally split, he ran 5km in 13:24 minutes. The Ethiopian team set a new world record with 1:57:04.

He was the Olympic Champion in Barcelona over 10K." At which Haile grinned and let his white teeth shine: "Do you mean the tall white guy who kept trying to catch up to me?"

The following year's racing would prove not only to be the most intensive of his career with 18 starts, but also one of the most successful. Despite various problems. It was the year of the World Athletics Championships. Jos Hermens met Haile in London at the Grand Prix and made two things clear to the talented runner ("I think he can become the best ever."): running has become a job that is now all about money. Before the World Championships in Stuttgart, he thought that Haile should run another race in the Zurich Grand Prix in order to be well-prepared physically and mentally with a good time. He would take care of the visa extension; it should not be a problem. Phone call to Addis Ababa to the Athletics Federation. They refused. Haile was in a dilemma. On the one side his Ethiopian employers and on the other his Dutch manager. The latter convinced him: "You will run a national record over 5K." Haile was finally persuaded, started in Zurich and finished in 13:05:39, a time never before bettered by any Ethiopian.

Clipping from the Journal "Laufzeit" of the Ekiden Relays 1992.

Äthiopischer Hattrick

Start-Ziel-Sieg beim 3. Ekiden Potsdam - Berlin

Äthiopiens Quintett war eindeutiger Favorit beim 3. Ekiden-Rennen vom Potsdamer Schloß Cecilienhof zum Brandenburger Tor nach Berlin. Fita Bayesa, Abraham Assefa, Worku Bikila, Haile Silassie und Addis Abebe teilten sich die Marathondistanz und wollten sich die 30000-Dollar-Siegprämie sichern. Dabei hatten sie sich diesmal stärkster Konkurrenz zu erwehren, denn 17 Nationalstaffeln, zwei gemischte Teams sowie 20 deutsche Ländervertretungen wollten die Sieger des ersten und zweiten Rennens jagen. Vor [illegible] Weltmeister Ke- [illegible] diesen Lauf [illegible] die

Start zum 3. Ekiden-Staffel-Rennen von Potsdam nach Berlin. Foto: O. Wessler

vorn. In 1:08:54 h siegte er in dem für alle Klassen offenen Lauf vor dem Potsdamer Wolfgang Köhler [illegible]:47) und Daniel Druska (BSV [illegible]

le/43:30) und Tibor Nitz[illegible] burg/44:15) verliefen si[illegible] der Position drei Kilo[illegible] Ziel. Sehr gut auch [illegible]

In Addis Ababa, they were angry and already guessed that the new star now wanted to shine in the Netherlands. So faces were all the more bewildered when Haile with the other Zurich participants appeared at the central Ethiopian airport. Thoughts that he could be banned from competing in Stuttgart were thwarted by his national record. Haile traveled to his first Senior World title race with a healthy self-confidence.

Track and Field World Championships 1993 in Stuttgart August 16th: 5K: 1st Kirui (Ken) 13:02:75, 2nd Gebrselassie 13:03:17; August 22nd: 10K: 1st Gebrselassie 27:46.02.

He competed in two finals. First up was the 5K; in the field was his old rival, Ismail Kirui. "There I made a mistake. Instead of worrying about him, I stuck to the heels of Fita Bayisa, the Olympic bronze medallist and Worku Bekila, the old warhorse. That is how the Kenyan stopped the Ethiopian 1, 2, 3." However, Haile was still second in this, his first Senior World Championships and received the Silver medal.

Plans for the 10K were already encroaching on his joy. He absolutely had to win it. So in the final he stuck to the heels of joint-favorite Kenyan Moses Tanui. Everything seemed to run as expected, in the truest sense of the word. Until in a bit of jostling Tanui lost a shoe and blamed Haile behind him by pointing at him angrily. "He said I stepped on his foot, but I would have noticed." Disqualification? Problem for the track officials. Haile did not let this stop him finishing. "If I was going to be disqualified, at least it would be as the winner." And Haile won. The Kenyan protested. The officials then watched film of the critical phase several times, but could see no evidence of irregularity or unfairness. Haile became World Champion in Stuttgart!

This news arrived home immediately and was celebrated by almost everyone from the Prime Minister in Addis Ababa to the shoe-shine boy in Axum. The world was amazed. For the first time, titles like 'running prodigy' or the 'running phenomenon' appeared in the media. When Haile landed back home, his family and friends had prepared a welcome party. Federation officials though kept a low profile. There was a rift between them, not least because of the plans of his Dutch manager, but also because of his own ideas about races and appearance and prize money. It has never really been healed.

The world record hunt began in Hengelo

For June 4th, Jos Hermens had prepared the first world record race for the new world champion. The place: Hengelo in the Netherlands, was already known by the manager in a running context. The Rotterdam Marathon and the Adriaan Paulen Memorial both traditionally used the venue. Hermens had extensive experience of organizing races of all distances and knew how to use pacemakers, how to create a good atmosphere in the stadium and had interested sponsors for such earth-shattering. A 5K world best time was long overdue. The last one dated from 1987: 12: 58:39 by the Moroccan Said Aouita. Haile was observed closely in the preceding months by Hermens and eventually asked: “Do you think we can give it a try?” He did not hesitate: “You know, training is going very well, I feel great. I am convinced that I can break the record.”

Haile Gebrselassie – world champion over 10K

After 3,000m, the pacemakers dropped out and left the track exhausted. Haile now battled on alone, lapped the other participants and showed a talent (which would also prove decisive in many later trials) for running alone against the clock, relentlessly against it and against himself. When he reached the finish line, frenetically fired up by the stadium announcer and the spectators, for the athlete from Addis Ababa was still quite a novelty, the Moroccan’s best time was improved by 1:43 seconds.

That was the first in an almost unbelievable world record hunt for Haile, who one year later in the same place was continued over 10K. This time in front of an absolutely packed stadium, also including excited Ethiopians who lived in the Netherlands and did not want to miss the new star from their homeland. One of the pacemakers for this memorable race in Hengelo was also Worku, now one of Haile's best friends, and kept him on time for more than 14 laps. This time, Haile broke Kenyan William Sigei's record by almost six seconds. The Ethiopians in the stands could not stay in their seats. They ran with their country's flag onto the track and carried it on their shoulders around the stadium.

Haile's first world record: 5K in 12:56.96 (Hengelo, June 4th 1994).

The man from the East-African Highlands' increased his tally of world records and world best times to more than two dozen by the end of 2007, over distances between one mile and the Marathon. This included running a distance of 21,285m in one hour.

Just this total, bordering on a running history phenomenon, understandably gave many people the reason to write or talk euphorically about a 'running prodigy' or 'the greatest'.

In the pre-Olympic year of 1995, Haile Gebrselassie raced no less than fifteen times, including middle distance races over 1,500m and over 12,060m cross-country. In Gothenburg, Sweden, he successfully defended his World Championship title. Was he now starting to collect Gold medals like other people collected stamps? He was not sure how he should celebrate such a collection. As World Champion in Stuttgart he had won a Mercedes and now in Gothenburg a second one. Everyone else jumped for joy, but Haile was rather annoyed: "I didn't have a driving license, and I actually didn't want to drive a car, just to run. I always told myself that a car makes you lazy."

And so he left the two cars in Addis Ababa in a car park with an attendant. He only wanted to deal with them after Atlanta. The Olympics had right of way.

3 Three-time Olympian: Atlanta, Sydney, Athens

Endurance

No film has reflected Haile's ascent to Olympic victory in Atlanta as emotionally as that of American director and screenplay writer Leslie Woodhead. Titled "Endurance", it stars Haile Gebrselassie himself, with his nephew, Yonas Zergaw, playing him as a teenager. Until the Olympic 10K, the producers were actually not in agreement as to who the hero of the film should be: Haile or Paul Tergat. They had watched both in the run-up to the Games, as they believed that the fight for Gold would only be between Kenya and Ethiopia. Gebrselassie had recently jumped to the top of the runners' rankings after his world record; Tergat had boasted an impeccable cross-country winning streak before Atlanta, even though he had kept a low profile in the Kenyan Championships. Paul or Haile? Director and cameramen prepared everything in duplicate so that they could decide between them after the day of the final on July 29th, 1996.

Paul Tergat or Haile Gebrselassie. Who wins – the Olympic final and the title role in the film?

Neither the filmmaker nor even Paul Tergat could have anticipated the drama that unfolded in the days before the semi-finals, the qualifying round of the men's 10K.

They had no idea that in the single room Haile had organized for himself in the athletes' village in Atlanta, his foot hurt. A blister was developing on his left big toe, which is not impossible as this is a perennial runners' problem. We know that carelessly pulled on socks could have been the cause, but the Ethiopian didn't wear socks. The blister grew bigger and its owner made a mistake, he picked at it. The small wound got infected and soon no shoes would fit, and even wearing a larger size did not help. Haile was both horrified and confused. "Have I flown to Atlanta just to give up because of a blister?" and "My God, what have I done wrong?" All of Ethiopia was expecting him to win, Haile knew that and absolutely did not want to disappoint. Everyday, Alem called him and suspected nothing. She wanted to encourage him to run well in his first Olympic appearance. "Haile, I already have our rings. We agreed, when you return…" Both had agreed to get married after Atlanta, while still in Bole Airport. Of course, Haile had been planning to be wearing a Gold medal around his neck. And now this big, painful blister!

The doctor that his manager, Jos Hermens called had only one piece of advice: don't run any more; rest, ideally in bed. The Kenyan already wondered why he never saw the world record holder. "Haile runs very early in the morning when you are still sleeping", the Manager replied evasively.

The film "Endurance" starring Haile Gebrselassie (Haile), Shawanness Gebrselassie (Haile's mother), Yonas Zergaw (young Haile), Gebrselassie Bekele (Haile's father), Alem Tellahum (Haile's wife);
Director and screenwriter: Leslie Woodhead,
Cinematography: Ivan Strasburg.
80 minutes long. A Hollywood production.

Nobody could avoid the semi-finals though. Anyone who does not start is already out, even if he leads the world rankings. "Doctor," asked Haile finally, "can I run anyway?" The doctor pointed out that it was his responsibility and that he would have to put up with the pain for almost half an hour. "Good" decided Haile, "I will race. I will ignore the pain." On the telephone he still did not tell Alem anything about his problems: "Everything's ok, now things are really taking off. You can rely on me." And at the press conference in front of the inquisitive media representatives he laughed as usual, not only at some unnecessary questions: "Yes, this is my first Olympics, yes, I feel good, yes, of course I want to win."

The pressure grew. The pain did not subside, but the expectations increased and with them his nervousness. When on the day before the 10K final his Ethiopian training companion Fatuma Roba kissed the tartan track of Atlanta after a supreme Marathon victory, it was finally clear to him what a return home without the Gold medal would mean. Fatuma was the first African woman to win Olympic Gold, which was immediately compared to Abebe's historic victory in Rome.

The all-deciding race

July 29th, 1996, 10K final, 77°F (25°C) at more than 80% humidity, highly-charged atmosphere

As expected, the drama is building up in the Olympic Stadium of Atlanta. Right after the start, Haile slots into sixth place, all the while keeping his eye on Paul Tergat. All the Kenyans flank him like bodyguards, giving the second Ethiopian Worku Bekila, a proven warhorse, no chance to support Haile. Haile knows that he must now fight alone for his country. Up to kilometer eight, no problem, but then he feels his foot pain again, almost overpoweringly, but does allow himself to notice. Neither can he, for in the lead, Tergat is increasing the tempo. The last two kilometers in 5:05 minutes! When the Kenyan kicks, only Haile can follow, 200m in 29 seconds. Moroccan Salal Hissout, long considered joint-favorite misses the crucial moment. A little later, Tergat looks around, probably to reassure himself of victory, but he has not been able to shake off Gebrselassie. "I didn't think any more about the pain, nothing except that believed in my willpower and my finishing speed", said Geb later. 450m before the finish, he makes his move suddenly and decisively. When another runner has to be lapped, he swerves and runs past the Kenyan leader with giant strides. For a moment it looks as though Tergat is standing still. No matter how hard he tries, Haile Gebrselassie can no longer be beaten, he looks around once on the finishing straight and then knows: I have won!

Haile Gebrselassie, Olympic 10K Champion in Atlanta in 1996

Olympic duel between Haile Gebrselassie and Paul Tergat in Atlanta

The stadium goes wild. Ethiopian spectators give him the green, yellow and red national flags. Haile tears the shoes from his feet, and anyone who looks can see that one toe is bleeding. He runs barefoot, still laughing as he passes the stands. The dream he has had since childhood has come true. He has emulated Miruts Yifter's Olympic victory in Moscow, he has not let his countrymen down, kept his promise to Alem and also finally convinced his father of his ambitions. There is only one cloud to spoil his joy: he would have loved his mother to be able to experience Atlanta. As the national anthem honored the winner, the smile disappeared from his face for a few seconds and gave way to a few tears.

The tall Paul Tergat, a gentleman also in defeat, congratulated the victor. Manager Hermens took the first congratulatory telephone calls behind the scenes. In Ethiopia, according to cautious estimates, tens of thousands of people poured onto the streets of the cities and villages to celebrate the Olympic success of Haile Gebrselassie exuberantly and at length. A local newspaper rhapsodized: "A shining light is born!"

1996 Atlanta Olympics, men's 10,000m:
1st Gebrselassie (Eth) 27:07.34
2nd Tergat (Ken) 27:08.18
3rd Hissout (Mor) 27:28.59
4th Nizigama (Bur) 27:33.79
5th Machuka (Ken) 27: 35.08
6th Koech (Ken) 27:35.19
The Ethiopia Fatuma Roba won the women's marathon in 2:26.05 on July 28th, one day before Haile.

Notable achievements after Atlanta

The enthusiasm after the Atlanta Games did not subside in Ethiopia. The Gold medals of Fatuma Roba and Haile Gebrselassie, plus the bronze of Gete Wami, had brought euphoria to the country that was otherwise only the subject of negative headlines: drought, floods, famine, wars. International statistics showed that Ethiopia was the poorest country in the world. Where were the reports about the beauty and friendliness of the people on the Horn of Africa, about the solidarity of the multi-ethnic state, the natural phenomena, the religiosity and unique history, dating back to the origins of mankind?

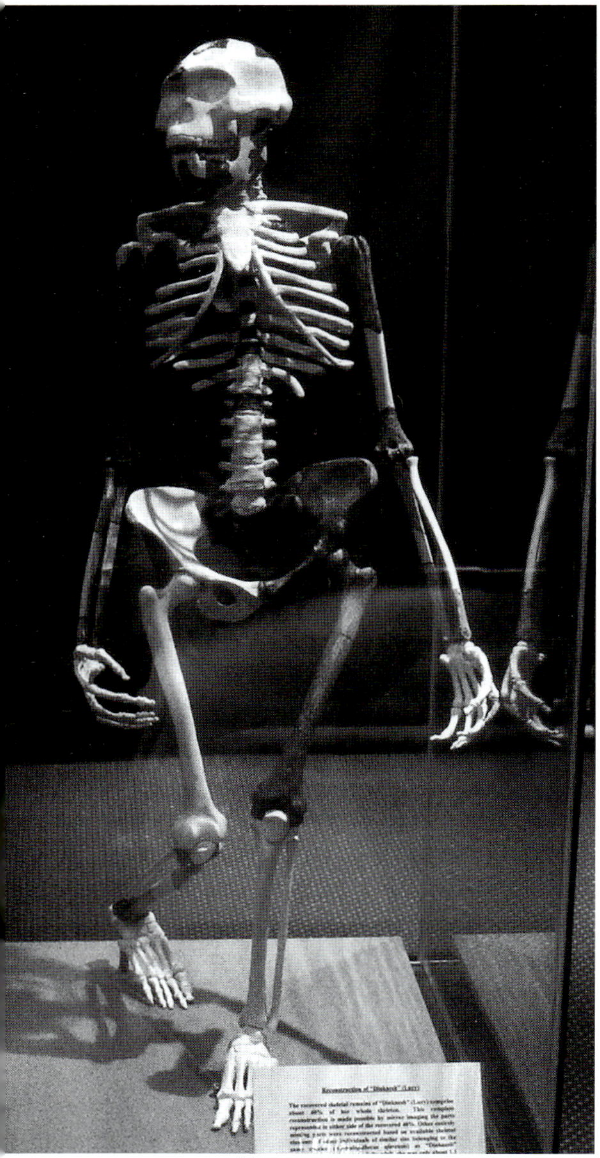

This is where "Lucy" was discovered, the oldest woman in the world, who walked upright three million years ago and was the first to run upright. A Beatles song (Lucy in the Sky with Diamonds) had inspired the archeologists in the Awash Province to choose this name; the Ethiopians called her "Dinkenesh", the "first beauty".

And now heroes were returning home, once more attracting international attention to the "roof of Africa". They were forced to spend two days in Frankfurt am Main because of an extraordinary order that had come from Addis Ababa: we need some time, we want to prepare a proper welcome for you.

Was Lucy the world's first runner?
In 1974, Dr. Donald Johanson from the University of Cleveland, USA, discovered the skeleton of a human who walked upright about 3.5 million years ago. Called "Dinkenesh" by the Ethiopians, which became "Lucy" because of the Beatles song "Lucy in the Sky with Diamonds". The long-sought missing link between apes and humans.

Thousands and thousands then feted the medallists from Atlanta with unbelievable enthusiasm all the way from Bole Airport to Meskel Square. But if you ask Haile today what he remembers most about landing in Addis Ababa, he would say Alem.

While still at the airport, an Orthodox priest led the woman in her celebratory champagne colored gown to the new Olympic champion, who was wearing the Gold medal around his neck like a cross. Surrounded by the entire Gebrselassie family, Alem handed over the gold rings, thus making their agreed engagement reality. The marriage between Alem and Haile did not take place, as it has often been reported, on this or the following day, but three months later. The exact number of wedding guests has never been ascertained, but has been estimated at 3,000.

The years between Atlanta and Sydney have often been written about. They are undoubtedly some of the 'wonder runner's' most successful. Coached by Dr. Woldemeskel Kostre and managed by Jos Hermens, almost everything he did was a success. He improved world records between 2 miles and 10K and defended his World Championships title. This brought him considerable wealth, which he invested not abroad but in his homeland. But Haile highlights one result from the year 1998, that means more to him than any prize money or trophies: the birth of his first daughter, whom he named Eden.

As he was being crowned World Champion for the ninth time in Seville on August 24th, 1999, again in front of Paul Tergat, he looked forward confidently to Sydney, where the Summer Olympics were scheduled to take place the following year. He had not idea after the Spanish fiesta how rocky the road to the Australian final would be.

After a nightmare: triumph by 9/100

Already at the end of 1999, the first problem emerged. Haile's physiotherapist, a Dutch specialist selected by Jos Hermens, had discovered the spot. The tissue of the right Achilles tendon was getting thicker and thicker. When Haile saw the Doctor, he had only one prognosis: operation. The patient did not want that though, as he saw his hopes for his second Olympic Games disappearing with it. "I want to run and win," and he repeated it again: "run and win." Anton Engels, the physiotherapist, placated him: "I will do all I can so that you do it. You must decide though." For weeks, he treated Haile round the clock; he even moved to Addis Ababa and lived with the Gebrselassies.

The outdoor season went very well, with Haile entering 5K races in preparation for the 10K in Sydney. Three easy victories before the last test, the Zurich Grand Prix, followed. If the pain already in the previous races had been noticeable, it culminated in Switzerland. Haile won, but what came afterwards he will never forget: He could no longer walk; he just had to sit there. He waited like this in the Zurich stadium until his rivals were out of sight. Had they noticed anything? They had, but they didn't mention it to him. Jos Hermens and Anton Engels helped Haile back to his hotel, above all protecting him from the press.

On his return home, he avoided everyone. He seemed irritable, unrecognizable as the always smiling running star with his familiar calm and contemplative nature.

But he thought that his second Olympic dream was over. "It was the worst time in my life, really. I did not know what to do. I couldn't sleep and didn't want to see anybody. I argued about nothing, even with Alem. What could I do?"

Sydney 2000 Olympics, men's 10K:

1st Gebrselassie (Eth) 27:18.20,
2nd Tergat (Ken) 27:18.29,
3rd Mezgebu (Eth) 27:19.75,
4th Ivuti (Ken) 27:20.44,
5th Korir (Ken) 17:24.75,
6th Berioui (Mor) 17:37.83.

The women's 10K was won by Derartu Tulu in 30:17.49.

After a failed endurance test that drove the pain up to new levels, at first he said: "I'm pulling out of Sydney." The last words of the Deputy Sports Minister, which went something like this, had tipped the balance: "Even though you are injured now, I am convinced that you will win if you race in Sydney." And so Haile flew to Australia. After a month without training, but newly motivated by the expectations of his countrymen and his own dream, that he wanted to fulfill after four years of the hardest training and numerous world records: to become Olympic champion for the second time.

Derartu Tulu, Olympic 10K champion in Sydney.

After the qualifying race in the Sydney Olympic stadium, which he won, he had to go straight to bed. The physio had three days to take care of him. He did not look good, so even an optimistic manager like Jos Hermens, himself a former world class distance runner, had little hope. But the little Ethiopian with the big heart stood up on the final day and showed everyone his smile. During the warm-up, Paul Tergat came up to him: "Haile how are you?" and Haile, trying not to limp or to give anything away, replied: "Fantastic!"

Olympic duel between Haile Gebrselassie and Paul Tergat in Sydney

Paul Tergat, now the eternal runner-up, wanted to turn the page at last this time. The Kenyan, almost a head taller than his Ethiopian rival, had never trained so hard, up to 200 miles per week. His form, as he himself admitted, had never been as good as before the 2000 Olympics. He made no secret that he had his first real chance against a diminished Haile Gebrselassie.

September 25th, 2000, Olympic Stadium in Sydney, Australia
10K final, 112,000 spectators

Tergat leads from the start, supported by his countrymen Korir and Ivuti. Gebrselassie sticks to his heels. They cover the first half of the race in 13:45 minutes, i.e. not too fast. Haile takes the lead twice, to prevent a faster pace. Nobody knows that the Olympic champion feels bad after seven kilometers; less from the pain in his toes than from a sudden breathlessness. The nagging question: "is it all over now?" lasts only seconds, then he feels able to cope again

HAILE GEBRSELASSIE

Just before the final show-down between Gebrselassie and Tergat.

on this track. When four laps before the finish, Paul Tergat sprints off, 200m in 29 seconds, only Haile can follow. "My only thought, you must wait." Then the Kenyan set a pace as though the finishing line were looming up in front of him, but he still couldn't shake the Ethiopian off. The little man with the letters "Ethiopia" above his vest number 1658 was still behind him. On the finishing straight, with 50m to go, the vest with the red stripe down the sides drew level. Haile Gebrselassie fought against Paul Tergat with all his remaining strength. "I couldn't think any more, just sprint. I felt as though I was running beside myself. It was a magical finale." Haile wins by nine hundredths of a second, the thickness of a vest!

The more than one hundred thousand spectators cheered both runners enthusiastically. Haile Gebrselassie's dream had come true. The second Olympic Gold. He limped around the lap of honor, then he was carried on people's shoulders around the track, that was bubbling like a cauldron. The headlines surpassed themselves again later

They now called him 'the greatest runner of all time.'

Haile Gebrselassie, Olympic Champion 2000 in Sydney over 10,000 m

Five miles in three hours

October 6th was a day that the heroes of Sydney will never forget. Jet fighters escorted the Ethiopian Airlines plane. Thousands of people were already thronging the airport, the largest one in Africa. Everyone from in and around Addis Ababa wanted to see their stars and cheer them. This Olympic team was the most successful in the history of Ethiopian sport. They brought home eight medals, long removed from luggage and hung around their necks, including Gold for Abera Gezaghegne, Deratu Tulu and Haile Gebrselassie. Garlands of flowers were placed around their necks while they were still on the airplane steps. The drive to the city stadium, only five miles long, took an incredible 3 hours. The enthusiasm knew no bounds. People not only thronged the wide streets, but were also perched in trees, bridges, balconies and roofs. They danced and sang, as is the custom everywhere in Ethiopia at times of great joy. Police escorted the vehicles on horses and motorbikes. "It was indescribable", Haile still remembers today with a certain shiver of excitement. "After Atlanta, our welcome was already fantastic, but the one after Sydney surpassed everything. We were completely overwhelmed." It was not only Haile's second victory that caused the Ethiopians to celebrate so exuberantly. Tulu, the girl from Bokoji village, who back in Barcelona was the surprise first female African winner of the 10K, had now won a gold medal again eight years later. She was crowned the 'running queen' by her compatriots. Abera Gezaghne was the name of the third Ethiopian Marathon champion, a particularly prized success after Mamo Wolde's 32 years earlier and the legendary Abebe Bikila in the 1960s.

A special stop of the vehicle convoy showered with flowers was required, when a banner "Welcome Haile Home" was spotted, upon which the hero of Sydney jumped from the open-topped car and hugged the banner-bearer, who was none other than Alem. After all the welcome receptions of this day, he spent the night alone with her in an unknown hotel, while the festivities continued among family and friends. Ethiopians know how to party long and hard.

One month later, the exceptional runner opened a Kindergarten that he had had built in Bahir Dar on Lake Tana, near the source of the Blue Nile. He gave it the name of his mother: Ayalech. In Addis Ababa he founded a Global Adidas Club, where 35 of the most promising running talents could train and be looked after free of charge. So they

Distinctions for Haile Gebrselassie: World Athlete of the Year 1998, Honorary Ambassador of the United Nations, recipient of the Olympic Order, three times honorary Doctorate (Dublin, Leeds, Jimma). In Addis Ababa a street is named after him: Haile Gebrselassie Street, appointed Major in the Police.

Rapturous welcome home from Sydney.

could follow in his footsteps. The "city of the new flower" honored the now Major in the Police by naming a street after him: "Haile Gebrselassie Street", a long street that was previously named for Eritrea.

However, all honors and hoopla must come to an end. Especially for one who, even though he was now a national hero, for better or for worse must now go under the surgeon's knife.

Year of hope and trepidation

Haile had to complete a tour of Europe before he found the right surgeon. Jos Hermens organized an itinerary of specialists in Finland, France and Switzerland, all in a few days, accompanied by Anton Engels, his trusted physiotherapist. The Olympic Champion's bag was full of entry visas and plane tickets. Haile, although more than used to exertion, was soon in a cold sweat. When the manager conjured yet another doctor out of his address book, he waved

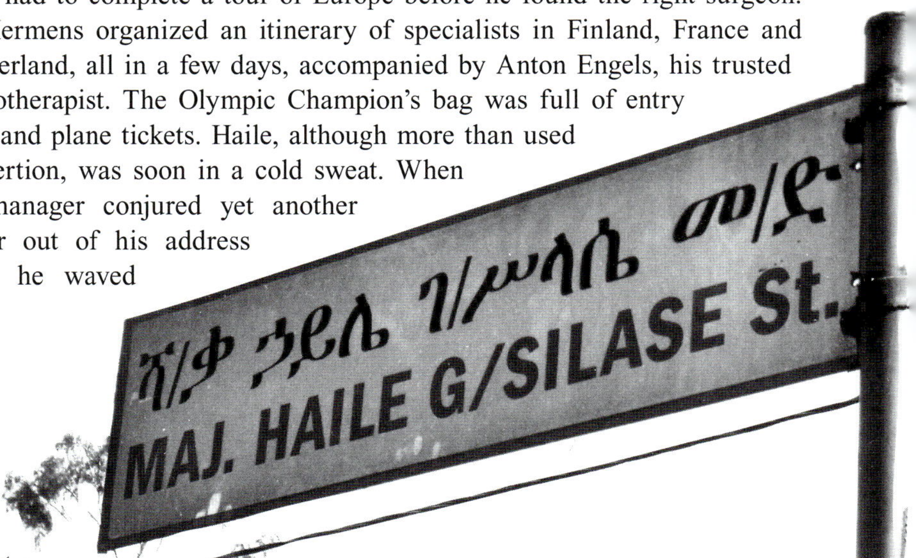

Dedication of a new street.

him away nervously. “Why don’t we go to the Swiss doctor, he seemed impressive…” Haile pleaded, and Anton Engels flew with him to Berne. At Dr. Peter’s he finally went on the operating table and his Achilles tendon went under the surgeon’s knife (under local anesthetic).

A stamp was issued in Ethiopia to commemorate the honor “World Athlete of the Year 2000”.

The Swiss doctor was satisfied afterwards; he prescribed gentle therapeutic exercises and discharged his high-profile patient within ten days, in which he clearly remembers that he spent most of his time in bed drawing pictures for Alem.

In the arrivals hall in Addis Ababa, brothers, sisters and wife waited impatiently for the homecomer. When he came through passport control bandaged and on crutches, their faces fell. Alem shrieked in horror: “What have they done to you? You’ll never be able to run again! Haile smiled shyly and pointed out: “Look, I can walk again” and convinced his welcoming committee that the crutches and bandages were only needed for convalescence. “You’ll see, I’ll soon be running again.”

The domestic therapy program of the Bern doctor prohibited running for six weeks, but allowed aquajogging, cycling and light weight training.

Haile cut it short; after half the prescribed time, he was already back running again.

Half Marathon debut 2001: August 26th Ethiopian Half Marathon Championships, 1:04:34, 1st place. October 7th, World Half Marathon Championships, Bristol, England, 1:00:03, 1st place.

Rapturous welcome home from Sydney.

In his new competition plans, he included the World Championships in Edmonton. Of course, he sometimes thought way ahead, to Athens 2004. However, for a long time he really did not know how his career would develop after the Achilles tendon operation. "God will help me," he sometimes told himself, and as a deeply religious Amhar, he was also convinced of it. Hope and trepidation featured heavily in the coming months.

When he landed in Edmonton in August, he was forced to take to his bed again with fever. But when his body temperature was back to normal again, he went to race. He finished the World Championships final in 3rd place. Coach and manager considered that to be a good comeback after only three months' training. His fans at home saw it a little differently: was the wonder runner's time over? In the last four year, Haile had always won; apart from two second place middle-distance finishes, i.e. an unbelievable 52 times.

Marathon return 2002 April 14th, London Marathon, 2:06:35, 3rd place.

Soon though, his fans were happy again and followed with interest his half marathon debut, which was apparently a resounding success. World Champion at his first attempt in Bristol and a year later a victory in the Lisbon Half Marathon, which was famous for being the world's flattest. When it became known that the 10K Olympic Champion had entered the London Marathon, people started placing their bets: Haile was moving up to the blue ribbon event. In April 2002, he gave the 26 mile 385 yard distance another try after 14 years, after many days of long, hard training, and finished third near Buckingham Palace, in a respectable first time of 2:06:35. But the voices in Addis Ababa again questioned why the superstar had not won there. "You have to live with it," says Haile, "People think you will always win because you have often won in the past. The same thing happens to other athletes. Sometimes I've even thought it would have been better not to take part than to lose, but defeat is all part of the game."

Two and a half months later, he was supposed to break the hour world record in the Dutch city of Hengelo. Instead, for the first time he pulled out of a race because of a torn muscle fiber.

Was it all really over now? Hope and doubt again. For six months. "Haile", said his Dutch manager, "there is actually a 10K race in the wealthy Gulf states in which they are offering $1million prize money for a new world record." Together they located Doha on the map, the capital of the United Arab Emirates. "Not bad." Said Haile, his humor returning. "If they thought that their money was safe in the safe, because I had not been winning any more recently, they may be mistaken." He trained for six months for the capital city of Qatar, with the desired success. Early that December morning, he finished 5 seconds quicker than the previous world best 10k time. The statistics differ over how many world records Haile Gebrselassie had now set. Now he didn't think about that though, but he was presented with a huge check, of which a lot was left over for his new business venture after pacemaker, manager and coach had received their share. "More than this breathtaking sum," he said with relief, "the most important thing for me was that I had got my self-confidence back."

A new star in the Ethiopian sky

He was not unknown to him. Since 1999, Kenenisa Bekele had been training in Dr. Woldemeskel Kostre's group, i.e. in the national squad, of which Haile was now the doyen. The same coach, the same manager. Kenenisa Bekele was also taken under the Dutchman's wing from the start. The king first met the new prince in November 2001 though, after he had just won the first Gold medal in the World Junior

Kenenisa Bekele.
Born June 13th, 1982 in Bekoj (Arsi Province), 5'3" tall, 119 pounds. Olympic Champion in 2004 over 10K and in 2008 over 10K and 5K, Olympic silver medallist in 2004 over 5K, World Champion over 10K in 2003, 2005 and 2007; World Cross Country champion from 2002-2006 and 2008. World records: 5K 12:37.35 (5.31.04, Hengelo), 10K: 26:20.31 (6.8.04 Ostrava), 26:17.53 (8.26.05 Brussels).

Cross Country Championships. Thanks to Haile, the 'Great Ethiopian Run' came into being in Addis Ababa with many sponsors, then still on the Bole Road right in front of his new business premises, and the expected hordes of participants flocked to it. The double Olympic 10K champion enticed people with a 10km race. Just the name Gebrselassie and a brightly colored finishers' t-shirt immediately got thousands of Ethiopians onto their feet. Especially, as intended, newcomers, but also all the ambitious runners who already dreamed of emulating their role model. Naturally, Haile competed in 'his' debut race and, as everyone expected, he won it. When Kenenisa Bekele crossed the finishing line 3 places behind him, he went up to him and congratulated him. They smiled at each other. The people, tightly packed along the normally very busy street that was cordoned off for the first time, cheered and clapped.

Kenenisa Bekele was a serial world cross country champion – here in the 2005 world championships.

Kenenisa was discovered playing soccer and persuaded to take up running. That was not too difficult for the physical education teacher in the small town of Bekoji, as running was the most natural thing in the world in this high province of Arsi, about 150 miles from the capital city. Kenenisa had, without knowing, already met his future idol as a schoolboy. Haile had to run 12.5 miles a day to school and back, Kenenisa 15 miles. He too had to drive the cattle into the pasture with his father and to bring the valuable water back from the watering place into the Tukul (the round, straw-covered hut) with his mother. He belongs to the proud Oromo tribe, who are usually tall and striking. When Haile was honored on the podium in Atlanta, Kenenisa was thirteen years old. Four years later, he was so inspired by the exciting Final in Sydney with Paul Tergat that he, usually so reserved, enthused: "When I saw Haile winning so bravely, I knew that this was what I wanted too." Reporters always asked him about Haile, and at first he admitted frankly that he wanted to be like him. But later on, he evaded this type of questioning more and more, and named Deratu Tulu as his role model (also from Bekoj) instead.

The new Ethiopian star not only twinkled, he very quickly sparkled with a radiance that few had anticipated. After moving to Addis Ababa, he was unusually quick to shine. Like a comet, he blazed across the running sky. One World cross country championships title after another, sometimes even both short and long at the same championships. But he also easily found his bearings on the roads and on the track. The first real dual with Haile, which he had wanted for so long, came in the year 2003, in the legendary Hengelo. Here he showed no respect, and was certainly not just a bystander on the track, but actively made his move. At the finish after 25 laps, he proved to be the better sprinter and prevailed, albeit by the thickness of a vest, but for the first time, over his hero.

Derartu Tulu:
born March 21st 1972 in Bekoj. 5 feet tall and 97 pounds. Olympic Champion in 1992 and 2000, Olympic bronze medallist in 2004. World Champion in 2001 (all over 10K).

The second victory over Haile took place in Paris and brought him still bigger headlines. One newspaper wrote: "Kenenisa Bekele ran away from his mentor and four-time Gold medallist with an ease that was never seen from the ‚Emperor‘ even at his best." Although Haile lost his World Championships crown over 10K, Ethiopia won three times. Such a triumph was unprecedented: Bekele – Gebrselassie – Sihine. All three possible World Championships medals went to the three representatives of the East African Highlands. The new running star Kenenisa Bekele had now finally stepped out of the shadow of his hero Haile Gebrselassie. In the following year, in the weeks before Athens, he had two more highlights, after which many were already treating him as the new Olympic star. In a period of only nine days, he broke the world records over 5K and 10K..."I believe," Kenenisa said, who was otherwise not one to boast: "a new era has begun." And he added frankly: "Of course, I will be Olympic Champion, Haile's successor."

Jos Hermens described the new wonder runner as follows: "Kenenisa is different than Haile. He is not as open. He talks less and calculates more. With Haile I had more time to explain the world to him, teach him English and how to deal with the media, but with Kenenisa everything happened so fast that he was not prepared for some things, which caused misunderstandings. Particularly in financial matters, which Haile was not especially bothered about, he is very canny. He also belongs to the younger generation." Hermens even once rhapsodized: "He is not Jesus, he can't walk on water, but on earth he is unbeatable."

World Championships in Paris 2003:
10K: 1st Bekele 26:49.57,
2nd Gebrselassie 26:50.77.

Over 5K Kenenisa Bekele was 3rd (12:53.12).

And Haile? His comments were considered and therefore typical: "We can be glad to have such a runner. Ethiopia can count itself lucky that its supply of runners is not drying up. Kenenisa has a future in front of him, he is young and fast, as I used to be on the track." Then he added: "But I cannot be expected to rule the world of running forever." And after another pause for breath: "At least not on the track."

When Kenenisa waited for Haile…

Athens was supposed to resemble Paris as much as possible. Eventually, all three medallists from the Seine were all set for the city of the Acropolis. Kenenisa Bekele, Sileshi Sihine and Haile Gebrselassie. A trio the like of which the running world had never seen before. In the weeks before the Summer Olympic Games, the Ethiopian coaches and officials pushed these names up and down the 10K rankings with possible times as though on a chess board. This time they wanted eternal rivals Kenya to have no chances at all.

Things were to transpire a little differently.

When Haile moved into the Olympic village that glimmered in the Greek August heat, he started to limp again. This time the cause was his left Achilles tendon. It even hurt when he walked. Haile was distraught. At every Summer Olympics he had to struggle with injury. In Atlanta the sore toe, in Sydney the right Achilles tendon, and now in Athens the left one. "My God, what have I done to deserve this?" Even Jos Hermens suggested that he consider whether it would be better not to race. But Haile vigorously rejected all arguments. At the end of the day, he had won two Olympic finals in pain. At home a lot was expected of him, as always. Even the President phoned him up and asked how things were going. "Fine," said Haile and no one saw the expression on his face.

The team managers got together and gave him a new role in the Olympic final. He was not to run to win, but support his two teammates in the 25-lap race in their bids for Gold and Silver. With a heavy heart, he agreed. Goodbye to emulating Paris?

August 20th, 2004, 10K final in the new Athens Olympic stadium. Sold out for months.

Another hot, sultry evening. Nothing earth-shattering in the first 11 laps. Most of the time, the Ethiopians Haile Gebrselassie, Kenenisa Bekele and Silieshi Sihine control the race, until lap 18. Everything points to a finish like in Paris. But in the last two kilometers, Haile's Achilles tendon pain increases. Haile's rivals know from his face, which he was usually able to control in difficult situations, that something is wrong. Kiprop from Uganda overtakes him. Then also Tadesse from Eritrea. Kenenisa and Sileshi now have to decide the rest of the race by themselves.

Athens Olympics 2004
10K: 1st Bekele (Eth) 27:05.10,
2nd Sihine (Eth) 27:09.39,
3rd Tadesse (Eri) 27:22.57,
4. Kiprop (Ken) 27:25.48,
5. Gebrselassie (Eth) 27:27:70.

Meseret Defar won the women's 5K in 14:45.65.

An unfamiliar situation for both of them. Kenenisa Bekele runs a risk. He does not want to see his idol drop off the pace and he slows the race down. He waits for him. As he prepares for the fight to the finish, he is still looking at Haile. Only when he is forced to recognize that Haile can no longer keep up does he sprint off and away from him. The last three laps are a dual, in which Kenenisa Bekele clearly defeats Silieshi Sihine. Haile crosses the finishing line in fifth place and immediately says joyfully: "Gold and Silver for Ethiopia, that is absolutely fantastic." About himself, he only said: "That was the best I could do. I think I surpassed myself again today." Kenenisa Bekele, the new Olympic champion added another medal to his collection just a few days later. He won Silver in the 5K. Two Olympic distance medals for an Ethiopian, finally equaling the achievement of Miruts Yifter, who once electrified the young Haile on the radio. Miruts was 42 in Moscow, Kenenisa in Athens at 22 was almost half his age. What a country of legendary runners…

When Haile returned home to his friends in Addis Ababa, a famous Ethiopian singer wanted to console the most popular man in the land with a song. Tedy Afro had written a song about and for the three-time Olympian with his band, which won the hearts of all Ethiopians and which they still sing today.

HAILE GEBRSELASSIE

From the text of the song by Tedy Afro, written for Haile and the Athens Olympic Team:

Our people have blessed us and bid us goodbye
and put the flags of our land in our hands.

It would be a disgrace for us and our people if we came
home without Gold medals.

(vocalist) Haile to his teammates:
I have tried to run despite the pain to inspire you.
Now we have great confidence in you,
do what you have to do.

(vocalist) Ethiopian teammates:

It's very hard to reach the finishing line without you.

It's very hard, you are the source of my courage.

It's very hard,
I was looking for you.

It's very hard,
when I have to look back at you.

(vocalist) Haile: run fast,
we are all expecting victory.

Run fast,
our people are expecting victory.

Run fast,
nobody should be in front of you.

Run fast,
so everyone doesn't look back at me.

4 Of Running Encounters

At Haile's home again

I had never thought that this land of wonder runners would cast such a spell over me. Just one month after the first ever start by a German running group in the Abebe Bikila Marathon, in which I myself got to struggle with the altitude, I was landing once more in the light-flooded glass palace of the Ethiopian airport. Amanuel, the calm travel agency boss, smiled at us when I arrived in sunny Addis Ababa, slightly overtired, with Christel, our travel manager. As always, he asked: "How are you?" to which we always had to respond: "Fine", before we could start complaining about the turbulence of the Boeing over the Egyptian Western Desert. We wanted our second visit to include a couple of exciting trips and also if possible a marathon or even a half marathon. We had to find somewhere to build the school, a promise made by that German running group that had traveled through part of Ethiopia after its first meeting with Haile.

Amanuel did not need to evade the question about Haile, and whether he was in Addis. He was there. But where? After checking in at the Global Hotel and (naturally a must) making a real Ethiopian coffee, we went to look for him. I was clear about the order: first to the Alem Building, then information from the parking attendant who kept his boss's place free every day: he is not yet back from training. We travel towards the Megenagna Hill, which people call the "Athletic Village", because here many of the internationally successful athletes have used their prize Money to build splendid villas there, behind the simple, but functional corrugated iron shacks, mostly behind walls. There could not really be a greater contrast,

Haile at home

but it had not turned into a subject of dispute that brought thousands of poor people out onto the hilly streets. The World and Olympic Champions are national heroes, revered, loved and appreciated. Running gods. Untouchable and yet accessible. A Haile Gebrselassie or a Kenenisa Bekele do not need bodyguards. They have become the pride of this long-suffering land. A plaster covering many wounds.

We got lost in the hilly landscape studded with huts and palaces, stopped and asked for directions. Exactly at that moment, an old Mercedes came around the bend. "There he is, it's Haile", the boy in the faded sports shirt said delightedly and waved to his illustrious neighbor. Haile stopped, smiled his world-famous smile and hugged us according to the national custom, shoulder to shoulder. He was on his way to train in the Entoto Hills. He thought quickly. "Shall we meet in the office in two hours?"

Then something unexpected happened that brought our conversation to an abrupt end. About 60 yards above the unmade road, a little gir had fallen and was crying. Haile left us standing there and immediately sprinted off to the little one, wiped the blood from her face and shouted for the mother. Only when she had been found and he was sure that the little girl did not need to be taken to hospital, did he return to us. "So, it was a good thing that I was here."

In the Alem Building on the Bole Road

You can't miss the Bole Road. It is the access road from the airport to downtown Addis Ababa, so can be considered the flagship of the new, growing metropolis of Addis Ababa. Numerous tower blocks, modern shops and all kinds of cafés, bistros and restaurants line the wide boulevard, which is also referred to as "Africa Avenue" in the city map. It is tough to drive here and people usually look for short cuts down the unmade side roads. There the contrasting image of this very young capital city can be seen: the poorest people's dwellings, hidden in a lot of greenery, alongside impressive, stone villas, often side by side. There are no real slums; Ethiopia really is the cleanest country in Africa. There is no comparison with the ghetto-like townships in South Africa or Kenya. In parliament, the politicians debated the problem of plastic bags: should we ban or limit their use?

The Bole Road
(also known as Africa Avenue) starts at Bole International Airport in the south east of Addis Ababa and ends at Meskel Square. It is a modern street with many shops, restaurants, bars, cafés and tower blocks. The Alem Building, which belongs to Haile Gebrselassie's family, can also be found here.

The Gebrselassie's Alem Building is formed of tower blocks situated opposite each other. The front one was constructed first. When we met Haile, this time in a black tracksuit, he invited us on a guided tour of his home. Almost underground, the Alem Fitness Center, a gym with the most up-to-date strength and endurance training equipment, with showers that he often liked to use after training and a sauna. Above it, with a terrace on the pavement, the Olympic Café, run by his brother Zergaw. On the walls, photos of Haile in Atlanta and Sydney. It seems to be hard to find a free table here. Everyone who frequents this popular place also hopes to meet the landlord. If they do, he will always chat briefly with them and let them take a photo with him. Haile cannot say no, and even enjoys his popularity. Up to the ninth floor, the space is used by companies: an Ethiopian Airlines agency, a bank, an insurance agency, a computer workshop…

The Alem Building

The British winner of the 1993 Hamburg Marathon, Richard Nerurkar, has also rented an office from Haile from which in his capacity as race director he organizes the Great Ethiopian Run and the Women's Race, also promoted as the Women's First Run. Countless thousands of participants start in both races, making them the most popular fun runs on the African continent. The ninth floor is used only by the Gebrselassie family. On the left side of the hall is their company, indicated by the sign: "Haile and Alem International PLC". Alem is in charge here. Haile has invested his money in many businesses: the construction of different kinds of houses, school projects in rural provinces, the buying and selling of SUVs. Campaigns against AIDS, famine and natural disasters are led from here. A resort hotel is even being built.

The door to Haile's office opens opposite. To reach it you must climb up step by step. Newcomers to altitude like us are already out of breath when we arrive. "The small lift there" explains our host with a twinkle in his eye, "is just for the disabled and pregnant women." In the outer office is the desk of Haile's personal assistant, a well-dressed, striking woman who, unlike almost all other Ethiopian women, had a serious expression on her

The Great Ethiopian Run is Africa's most popular 10km race, certified by the International Marathon Federation (AIMS). The charity run, under the aegis of Haile Gebrselassie, takes place every year in November and supports orphaned children. In Addis Ababa there is also a women's race over 5km, usually in March/April.

face. Probably as an initial deterrent, which is understandable. For locals and foreigners come and go endlessly every day to gaze in admiration at the national hero. They usually have to make do with the photos on the walls of Haile racing all over the world. On the desk is a large weekly diary, crammed full of appointments, and next to it a telephone. Who could invade this domain?

We entered the sanctuary, and from there went out onto the roof terrace. What an impressive panorama over the highest capital city in Africa. What an endless expanse, what a riot of color, what dense traffic. Addis Ababa seems to lie at Emperor Haile Gebrselassie's feet.

The second tower block had not yet been completed at the time of our visit, although we could already see work in progress on the 300-seat cinema. "The first private cinema in Ethiopia," as Haile liked to remind us repeatedly. We wanted to know what kind of films would be shown. "Funny ones of course. Like most of my compatriots, I love films that make me laugh." Now and then, Haile's film "Endurance" would also be shown, which was still a box office hit many years after its premier.

With Haile we drank the typically strong coffee (we would call it espresso) in "Alem 2", in one of the club rooms tastefully furnished with armchairs and low tables. Ethiopia is indeed said to be the original source of coffee, which was discovered in the 6th Century in the province of Kaffa. Legend has it that a shepherd was scared by his goats, which started to dance after eating a type of bean. A monk then used this amazing bean in order to stay awake for evening prayers. Merchants then traveled to Kaffa, roasted these beans and made them popular in Arabic countries. Initially, for us a bit of an acquired taste, we learned to enjoy the national drink of Ethiopia ourselves. With plenty of milk, for example.

Haile took his time. He stuck rigidly to his plans. The move up to the marathon distance was no longer a secret. After his second Achilles operation, he started to prepare himself physically and mentally for the Amsterdam Marathon. He thought Berlin seemed a good course: "I know that the course is flat and conducive to records." Above all he had good memories of Berlin from the Ekiden Relays and the "Internationales Stadionfest" ISTAF Berlin. "I miss your city."

He wanted to know our news. Christel, who had previously met him at a training camp for German runners, told him about the new Reichstag, the

Brandenburg Gate, the Gendarmenmarkt, the newly designed Pariser Platz and lively Potsdamer Platz and many more. In passing, she placed a photo on the coffee table of a gigantic Nicaraguan work of art pained on a Berlin house wall, and about the fundraising campaign that she personally had started in order to preserve it. "That is fantastic!" reacted Haile, reached spontaneously into his wallet and contributed a not inconsiderable amount of Ethiopian Birr to it. That is what he is like. If you told a German millionaire businessman en passant about such a venture, he would probably just say well done…

Meanwhile, Haile has also been recognized as one of the benefactors of Berlin Lichtenberg.

On the way to the Entoto Hills

To get to the highest land surrounding Addis Ababa, you need to go right across the city. After crossing Meskel Square, we turned into the wide avenue named for Emperor Menelik II, a boulevard of scented trees where the Africa Hall is situated– headquarters of the United Nations Economic Commission for Africa. Past the Imperial Palace, which today is the seat of government, in whose attractive environment unfortunately no photographs may be taken, further down King George Street to the Lion Zoo, founded by lion-fan Haile Selassie. Then Entoto Avenue starts, with Addis Ababa University.

It is said that if you drive quickly through the city, you can admire a wonderful "new flower" all around you. Addis Ababa does have its attractions, but also many shadow sides, and in its just over 100 years' history it has always been a city of contrasts, a city that people often only discover and love at second glance, but then enduringly so. In the impenetrable traffic jams, women with babies, young and old street children, cripples and homeless stretch out their hands to beg from the drivers. A daily fight for survival. If a six to eight-person household earned 400 Birr (about $40) per month, it would have enough to live on. Many foreigners are upset when faced with this poverty and think of how lucky they are and do not know to whom and how often they should give a Birr. If you are constantly confronted with this kind of situation you can no longer be at peace with yourself. Despite everything, none of the poor and poorest seems to have lost their smile.

Ethiopia is one of the poorest nations on earth. According to World Bank calculations, the national per capita income in 2003 in Germany was $25,250, while in Ethiopia it was $90 (rose to $159 in 2007).

The winding roads up to the peak of the Entoto Hills are the scene of another kind of suffering. Girls and women carry firewood from the remaining eucalyptus forests on their shoulders, half a hundredweight for maybe one or two dollars a

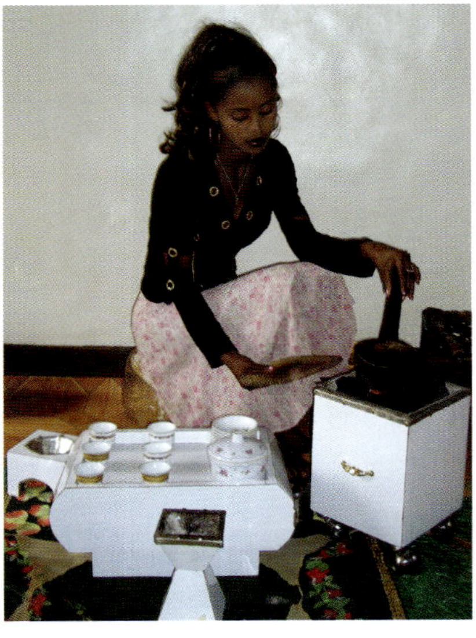

day. If they do it twice a day, they will have covered a distance of 20 miles between early morning and evening. The Athens Olympic champion 5K champion, Meseret Defar, is familiar with this drudgery. The only current female world class Ethiopian athlete, she grew up on the outskirts of Addis Ababa. She finally ran away from this burden because she wanted to become rich and famous like Derartu Tulu. Although her parents did not approve, she raced with the local girls for a bet, wearing the only pair of running shoes that actually belonged to her brothers.

The peak at 9,800 feet altitude offered a unique 360° view over the white-roofed capital city, whose greenery was only visible from above. How many inhabitants lived there is impossible to know exactly, but is estimated to be 5 million. There may well be more. The thinness of the air is palpable, as was its mid-June coolness also. On this highest peak, an artist has pitched his hut. Inside it, the walls are lined with Water colors and oil paintings from the cultures of different Ethiopian tribes. The prices are moderate, the artist enjoys every conversation and recounts that he wants to turn his little tin hut into a culture café. I take one picture of a fuelwood carrier away with me, as a souvenir of the trip to Mount Entoto.

From the peak of Mount Entoto, an artist, Washilum Asuake, presents a small art gallery.

Running in heaven

Menelik II founded the capital city of Ethiopia in the Entoto Hills,. That was back in 1892. In the St Maryam Church, not far from the peak, he was once crowned Emperor. Today it has a spacious car park on which not only the well-heeled city dwellers park their cars, but also the nation's running elite.

They meet up in the early hours of the morning, often still wrapped up in their green, gold, red tracksuits in the low temperatures. The sun twinkles right over the mountains. After an extensive stretching program, the long distance runners complete their mileage across the Entoto terrain, at altitudes of between 8,200 and 9,800 feet. "It is like running in heaven," grins Marathon coach Dr. Yilma Berta, with intentional ambiguity.

He does not avoid the question of a "normal" training week for Haile Gebrselassie. I learn that the Marathon runners have to turn up early in the morning at 7am and in the afternoon at 4pm and note Haile's program:

Monday: morning cross country run 110mins, roughly equal to 28km; afternoon another hour's running through the forest – 18km.

Tuesday: morning 20km in 80mins, afternoon gym work

Wednesday: run two hours on grass, 32km; afternoon light training for 72minutes, 18km.

Thursday: just easy morning training for 72 minutes, about 22km.

Friday: early road run over 30km, mid to high tempo; afternoon recovery.

Saturday: morning easy cross country training, 15km in 80 minutes.

Sunday: 8am: easy 15km run.

Total weekly distance run: 218km. Hard training that must be increased in certain periods.

Emperor Menelik II

The Entoto Hills are situated to the north of Addis Ababa, their 9,800 feet peak offers a fantastic view. Addis Ababa. These mountains were the origin of the founding of the capital city, when Emperor Menelik II allowed a fortified camp to be built there in 1878. In 1892, Addis Ababa replaced Entoto as the "new flower."

What is so special about Haile Gebrselassie, in the opinion of his discoverer and coach? “A common question,“ says Berta, then lists a few qualities that he considers essential, as well as talent and physical preconditions and hard training always at altitude: “Haile is very disciplined, extremely punctual, respects his coach and his training, thinks clearly, can get on with everyone, is not arrogant and everyone likes him.” Haile is known for his comprehensive stretching routine and for trying out all manner of possible and impossible exercises. “Who jumps rope regularly or rides a bike lying down?”

Dr. Woldemar Kostre, long-time Track and Field coach of the national team, is mainly responsible for designing the training programs of the Ethiopian running elite. His reign was rigorous, strict “almost militaristic,“ Haile once commented. Kostre himself said: Rigor is the prerequisite for discipline and discipline is the prerequisite of a good athlete. A duty that we all chose.” Of neighbors and eternal rivals Kenya,

He said: “There is too much democracy there, too much individuality, which is ultimately detrimental.” Team spirit and patriotism are apparently the keys to success.

All members of the national squad must live in Addis Ababa and train as a group. At least twice a week, all the squads run together, both men and women. Six weeks before a major international meeting, the athletes live away from their families, and home becomes the Ararat Hotel in the Entoto Hills. A visit to this small, but clean and well-maintained hostel, roughly equivalent to an American 3 star hotel, is worthwhile because of the impressive Ethiopian running history that adorns the walls. From here, the training paths rise higher and higher, through smaller reforested areas, up to altitudes of 9,800 feet. Anyone who cannot handle this challenge falls behind and drops out. Those who do make it are ready to break records.

Marathon training in the Entoto Hills.

Tolossa Kotu took over the post of Head Coach from Dr. Kostre in 2004. He is the man who discovered Kenenisa Bekele and guided him to Olympic victory. He agrees with Kostre's assessments and repeats: "We Ethiopians are more disciplined than the Kenyans and build on a natural training with a scientific background. The Kenyans run mainly for prize money; we run for our country."

In Ethiopia, altitude training is possible every day. Whether in the Addis Ababa stadium, the only one with a tartan track, in the cross country terrain of the Jan Meda race course, on the asphalted streets outside the city center, or just running in the mountains. Haile thinks; "Running at this altitude is an advantage for us. Training here is more intensive. If we then have the same conditions at low altitude as in the Highlands, we are quick. A lowlander needs a good two weeks for his body to adapt to our altitude."

Running facilities in Addis Ababa: the Addis Ababa stadium (also called Central Stadium), Meskel Square, the Jan Meda race course, the Entoto Hills, Street #1 to Sendafa, the terrain around the Ararat sports hotel.

After "running in heaven," Kenenisa, Derartu, Meseret and Haile met again at the tea stand in the car park near the small but magnificent Maryam Church, wrap themselves up again in their tracksuits and drive home by car to shower. More of the same in the afternoon…

Meskel Square – the world's largest sports ground?

The downtown proper starts where mighty Meskel Square (Cross Square) sprawls. It used to be called Abiot Square (Revolution Square), and many still call it that. Here the gigantic portraits of Lenin, Marx and Engels were displayed in the time of Mengistu Mariam. The square has a 100,000 person capacity, so that it is the ideal starting point for the Great Ethiopian Run in November with its 30,000 casual runners. Here at the start of Ethiopian spring on September 27th a huge stake with a cross at the top is burned, which is supposed to evoke the finding of the true Cross.

The runners of Addis Ababa meet here every day.

Tesfaye, of our partner travel agency, advised me to go with him to Meskel Square early one Sunday morning. At dawn, I stood with my camera much too early in front of the hotel entrance; I had to wait. However, I was surprised by what was already happening at this early hour in the still sleeping city. Men and women were jogging steadily along the dim, uneven streets in tracksuits and even in normal attire, in sports shoes as well as in sandals. Some interrupted their morning run and began to do exercises. Tesfaye, who had meanwhile arrived in his Toyota Jeep, just smiled. "Come to the square now."

A little later, I stood in front of the stands in the square and could hardly believe my eyes. I cannot deny that at first I was speechless. On my travels I had already experienced and seen many things. Masses of meditating men and women with warrior-like poses in China, countless groups of cross country runners on the jogging trails in Scandinavia. Hundreds of joggers in Central Park in New York. But it took me a while to comprehend what was going on here; the square, normally criss-crossed by very loud traffic and exhaust fumes was mostly cordoned off. Instead, countless improvised soccer pitches now took their place. The most striking thing though was the stands in the square, which looked like a giant amphitheater. On them, where according to the city guidebook statistics, 3,000 people stood during festivals, young and old were running in their hundreds. Each of the many wide, upward-sloping steps could be used for at least 400m. Back and forth, back and forth. In between them, groups with special exercise programs and step running, usually noisily directed by a chief counter. People were wearing clothing of all types of color and material. From new and borrowed tracksuits to short and long, mostly worn-out trousers, sweaters, well-worn shirts with sports goods firms' logos from all over the world and whatever shoes they owned. As I pushed between the runners, exercisers and jumpers with my camera, people gave me friendly looks but most of the Meskel athletes did not even notice me or stop what their were doing. They were mostly between 15 and 25, perhaps 30; few were older, but all were following in the footsteps of their heroes.

Training on Meskel Square.

One of them spoke to me, I remember very clearly; he was called Amare, aged 23. He wanted to know where I was from. Germany, I would really like to go there one day. Everyone must be rich there. To run? Yes, he said, to run and

also to live a little, have a better life. He was training to be a builder. At that time he lacked everything he needed to improve his 35 minutes best time over 10km, everything from good running shoes to shirts and shorts. Why did so many people train here daily and with so much enthusiasm? "They all want to be like Derartu Tulu or Haile Gebrselassie, rich and famous." On invoking his name, Ethiopian eyes not only shined here on Meskel Square, perhaps the biggest sports ground in the world. I later realized that the name Haile was here considered tantamount to holy.

Meskel Square (Cross Square): sports ground for hundreds of people.

Tesfaye then took me to Jan Meda, once the field of Emperor Janhoy. It is, he told me, the only large green space in Addis Ababa that has not been built on. It was once set up as a horse race track, but was and still is also used for the African cross country championships. On Sundays it is used by soccer players and joggers. As on the stands of Meskel Square, I was struck by the wide range of exercises being carried out. One man was counting out loud and diligently writing down the exercises performed, which included jumps and push-ups. Sunday is a sports day from sunrise to sunset.

Thousands celebrate the Festival of the Cross there every year.

When I got back into our SUV, my thoughtful guide wanted to know what I thought. I told him that in Germany we did have a really big running movement, but not such moldable running potential as here in Ethiopia. "Maybe you are too rich and that makes you lazy?" he finally reflected.

I just shrugged my shoulders. What will happen, I thought, when (as we really hope and wish) Ethiopia is no longer one of the poorest nations in the world?

In search of a childhood

Andy, for over two decades one of the most knowledgeable tourist guides, and Tesfaye, a car driver who was fazed neither by the chaotic city traffic nor by herds of cattle and sheep on the country roads, accompanied me to Asela. It was a long-held wish of mine to visit the place where Haile had grown up. Perhaps I would even get to meet his father?

Up to Nazareth in the south, we made our way through tailbacks of trucks, but on a very well surfaced highway, which, if you continued to the Ethiopian border, ran all the way to Kenya. However, after that we jolted along the remaining 60 miles to our destination. The road to Asela and further to Bekoji was being paved by roadworkers, with UN funding. Again and again we had to dodge not only donkeys and cattle, but also potholes down country lanes. My guides took it in their stride and preferred to point out interesting sights to me. For example, the red earth that contains as much iron as the water in the Arsi Highlands, and teff, the local cereal crop, which also contains iron. Asela is an important area of cultivation for wheat and barley, cereal crops that have been grown in Ethiopia for centuries. Many village huts displayed signs with a hand-painted cup or plate. These were signs for long-distance drivers letting them know that here they could get a drink of water or cola or even eat an Injera.

Ethiopia lies at an average altitude of 4,000 feet, so that pleasant temperatures prevail. In the Highlands of Arsi Province, mountains rise up to 13,000 feet. In this territory of the Oromo tribe, many world class runners have been discovered.

Asela itself is an unprepossessing little town, more of a big village, but still the principal town of this province that is home to the largest ethnic group, the Arsi Oromos. Andy informed me that Haile's father lived at the edge of the town. Behind a high wooden fence towered two satellite dishes, otherwise a very modest property.

A brother who had opened a successful restaurant in Asela with financial support from Haile directed us to the care home where father Gebrselassie was visiting a sick friend.

When we met him there, he gave us a rather cool, but not unfriendly, welcome. I had expected that, as from reports I knew that he still did not like nosy reporters and had even abruptly shut the door in the face of one of them. Andy must have put in a good word for me, for the "Ferendschi", the foreigner, who had traveled all the way from Germany. How was the 80-year-old Gebrselassie Bekele? Until the age of 50, he had been as strong as an ox, then he started to suffer from asthma, which was now getting worse. I asked him about Haile. At first he responded a little bitterly: "But he has been one of you for a long time, he's not mine any more." Then though, he told us proudly that only three days previously he had taken the bus to Addis Ababa and that he actually visited Haile at least once a month.

Was it a very hard time then in the village? He shook his head vigorously: "We did work hard, but we were not poor. We had many fields, even inherited

Father Gebrselassie Bekele.

plenty. We were a happy family." Yes, he was a strict father. "But I sent all the children to school and they all help me today."

He fathered 13 children, with two wives, one of whom had passed away. He was unable to tell us how many grandchildren he had straightaway. The conversation with father Gebrselassie gradually became more relaxed. He slept a lot, also sometimes watched the television that Haile had recently given him, or he traveled to Addis, as he had already mentioned. Finally he told us that although he had never learned to read and write, he could nevertheless write his own name. He then slowly and carefully wrote his name in my notebook: Bekele.

We then began our search the Arsi village in which the Gebrselassies grew up at an altitude of 6,500 to 9,000 feet. Tesfaye soon had to leave his Jeep at the side of the field and we continued on foot. The wheat had been vigorously threshed; two to three harvests are possible in the Highlands. Tukuls, the round farmers' huts, were dotted around some distance apart. The walls were made of acacia or eucalyptus wood and then they were covered in grass, with bamboo used for the roofs, ashes and cow pats for the floor and for rendering. In these Tukuls there is an open cooking area, a place for sleeping and living and a partitioned room for young or sick animals. No light, no windows and no running water.

The Gebrselassie family owned two huts, one of which was only used for cooking. Even this was considered to indicate a certain wealth. Andy tried to identify the location of their Tukuls with some older farmers. As that big, spreading tree to which Haile sometimes fled from his father's beatings could still be seen, we could all finally agree on a place.

The "autograph" of Haile's father BEKELE.

Before our return, we went to look for the school to which he ran every day with his books under his arm. Low, clean buildings from which the former schoolboy had had renovated and extended following his first Olympic victory. The headmistress did not mind showing us around, as long as we didn't interview the two remaining teachers who had taught during Haile's schooldays. We discovered photos and a few of newspaper clippings on the classroom walls, with which some pupils had followed the progress of the most famous schoolboy from Asela.

A few questions in Haile's Home

Haile never has time. That is understandable. Training twice a day, once a day in the office block, innumerable honorary memberships, invitations that he cannot refuse, traveling for races. And now me as well. "Haile, I just need one hour, maybe more, you know, for a few questions."

Countryside in the Arsi Province has been unchanged for centuries.

HAILE GEBRSELASSIE

The farm is still running as it was in his father's and grandfather's time.

Cautious attempt by telephone. In such situations, he cannot say no, it goes against his nature. "Good, let's meet at 2pm at my house, o.k.?"

The reunion was jovial, Haile this time was wearing a white tracksuit top, freshly showered and, as always, in an excellent mood. My voice recorder did not bother him, and we chatted freely, and only because of a heavyweight boxing fight on the TV screen, which was on around the clock here, did I once have to interrupt the conversation.

You are one of the most successful business people in Ethiopia. In a survey, you even placed third. How many lines of business does the Gebrselassie firm now operate?

First of all, running (grins). Of course, running is a business. The most important was though that we founded a family business "Haile & Alem International". When we started out, the company was quite small, a real estate business, sales and rentals. We now have several sites, in Bahir Dar, Asela, Nazaret. We have invested a lot of money in a 150-room tourist hotel. We also build condominiums and villas. In Asela, my hometown, we offer targeted support to talented child athletes, we gave money to build a gymnastics hall and for a cinema. You know, I love the cinema.

And can you manage so many businesses?

Sometimes I moan that we have too many businesses. It makes me quite ill (laughs). But I don't have to do it all myself, I have many associates. My brother Assafa manages all the construction work and my wife all the administration. Her father takes care of part of the car importing business. A total of 400 people work for us.

One of Ethiopia's riches is its contrasting landscape: the seemingly endless Highlands, the Simien Mountains that resemble the Grand Canyon, eight fascinating national parks and three animal reserves, extensive chains of lakes, the Great Rift Valley and the source of the Blue Nile, all so far unspoiled by tourists.

You've started many charity campaigns?
I work with several different organizations to fight AIDS and poverty together. We are also involved with the subject of heart disease. And, of course, sport.

What is your vision for Ethiopia?
I have very great hopes. Ethiopia will one day be a rich country, like America or Germany, I am sure of that. I don't think it will happen in my lifetime. Perhaps it will take 30 years, but my children or grandchildren will experience it.

How will this be achieved?
Much is possible. I grew up on the land, in the most basic conditions. In less than 20 years, I have become what I am today.

But not everyone is a Haile…
I want to tell you something. When I started running, there were very few runners. Look how many there are today!

You're right. This morning I saw 2 or 300 on Meskel Square.
You see, when I trained on that square, there were 4 people at most. That is just one example. That is why I think my country has a good future.

But not everyone can earn money from running…
Of course, I know that. But one thing that we really need is that everyone must sacrifice something. By sacrifice, I mean …I want to give you an example. Four or five hundred years ago, a bridge was built over the Blue Nile, the "Portuguese Bridge," which was constructed by many people who went through unspeakable suffering. But they did it. Sometimes you have to give something to get something. Everyone, from the President to the man in the street must give up something, for the poorest, for the country. Without such sacrifice there can be no success and no progress.

One of the paintings in the Gebrselassie's home – Haile as a young man.

Why is Ethiopia one of the poorest countries?

There are many reasons for this. Another example: Almost nothing is paid from abroad for the coffee from the "Land of Coffee." A coffee that has a unique, flowery aroma. 700,000 peasant families make a living from it and many go bankrupt and can no longer send their children to school. Droughts are also a factor. However, the biggest problem is that many farmers don't own their land, it belongs to the state, so they don't invest in it.

What should be changed internationally?

Many development projects suffer because the planners from the rich countries want to sell something expensive. We need help for important, basic things. I often say it like this: our people don't need to be given fish, they want to learn how to catch it.

What is your personal involvement?

I have become Honorary Ambassador for the United Nations, and when time permits, I travel into the countryside and give talks to young people, both about AIDS and my career. I want to be a role model for them, to make it clear to them that they too can achieve great things through hard work and training. Where necessary and useful, I also give money. That's how it is. Everything I do should be for my country.

I realized that, Ethiopia is a beautiful country…

It is fantastic here. People must see it. We have gorgeous scenery, mountains, the Great Rift Valley, the Nile Falls. Did you know that we have rainforests

Women firewood carriers near Welkite.

here and animals unique to Ethiopia? We have an ancient culture with the rock churches, the royal and imperial cities in the North. We have friendly and beautiful people and a pleasant climate. Muslims and Christians live peacefully side by side here. There are few countries like this in the world. But how many tourists come to visit us?

An entire nation runs, carries and smiles.

You are always laughing. That is how the world knows you. But honestly, do you ever get angry?

(Laughs again) Yes, of course, usually over little things. In sport I rarely get angry, for there are only two possibilities: either you win or you lose. I can get upset if people don't do their work properly, who don't take things seriously or if they are not punctual. If you have a job, then you must work, whether the boss is there or not. Or: when I am running through the forest and I see that trees are being felled, then I can get really angry. Many people know that now and put their ax down when Haile is running.

Yes, it is a pity about your trees…

Have you seen the big trees in our streets? A few years ago, I nearly punched a man. I was coming home from training about 6am, and I saw a guy with a saw next to these beautiful eucalyptus trees.

Have there been defeats that really bothered you?

Ah, yes, there've been a few. In Atlanta, I was especially sad when I could only run the 10K and not the 5K because of problems with my foot. Oh yes, and then also my third place in t he World Championships in Edmonton in 2001.

In the surroundings of Addis Ababa, Eucalyptus trees prevail. They were purchased at the start of the 20th century, when wood became rare in the city. In recent years, the Eucalyptus had to be replanted again as many of the fast-growing trees are chopped down and sold for firewood and construction.

Where does your laugh, your positive attitude to life come from?

(Haile becomes serious, reflective). It must be my character; I don't know where it comes from. My father was very strict. But my mother, who died young, was a very loving and warm woman. Yes, she had a similar character to me.

You are a family man, four children as of 2008…

Three daughters and one son, the youngest. My wife, my family is my foundation for everything that I have achieved. I thank God for them. The children are growing up well, but they really don't want to be runners. Recently my eldest daughter, Eden, told me: "You know Pop, I would like to be a famous runner like you." What should I say to that? She never will be. She can never be, because she didn't have the necessary background as I, or other poor athletes from the country, did. She is a spoilt city kid; she is driven to school in the morning and picked up afterwards. The richer people get, the lazier they are. However, I always say that not everyone can train for world records, but they can run and aim for personal records. I admire and respect all those who are still fit in their old age and run for their own health and enjoyment.

Waterfall in Awash National Park

Do you have heroes in your life?
At least two. Miruts Yifter, as you know. His two Olympic wins were the impetus for my career. We are now very good friends. When he comes from Canada, where he lives, to Addis Ababa, we always meet up. And then Nelson Mandela. When I met him in Cape Town, I was not yet famous; we did not talk to each other, but just shook hands, as he did with all the athletes. Later we corresponded. I was very moved when he sent me his book with a personal dedication inside: "Your successes are an inspiration for the whole continent. I hope we shall meet again one day before I die."

Ethiopian running greats from different eras: Sileshi Sihine, 10K Olympic runner-up in 2004, Miruts Yifter, Olympic Champion over 5K and 10K in 1980 and the women's 5K African champion Meselech Melkamu.

Trade
DENIM
mark

Ethiopia:
"the land of many smiles."

Brief history of Ethiopia

Around **1495BC**, the Egyptian Pharoah Hatshepsut undertook a sea voyage to Punt.

In the **1st century AD**, the Kingdom of Axum was founded. Abyssinia is created.

330	Christianity becomes the state religion under King Ezana. Greek and Egyptian influences.
625	Start of Islamization.
	In the 12th century King Lalibela had the 11 rock churches built.
1636	Founding of the capital city in Gondar.
1889	Italian invasion in the North and founding of the colony of Eritrea.
1865-1913	Emperor Menelik II.
1892	Founding of Addis Ababa.
1930 – 1974	Emperor Haile Selassie.
1935	Italy attacked Ethiopia and occupied the country until 1941.
1960	Abebe Bikila became Africa's first Olympic Champion by winning the Marathon in Rome.
	In the same year, attempted coup d'état against Emperor Haile Selassie.
1974	Revolution and deposal of Emperor Haile Selassie.
	The bones of "Lucy" (Denkenesh) were found, a 3.5 million year old skeleton.
1977	Colonel Mengistu Haile Mariam seized power and in 1987, declared the People's Democratic Republic of Ethiopia.
1991	After riots and civil wars, Mengistu Haile Mariam fled to Zimbabwe.
1992	Derartu Tulu became the first female Olympic champion over 10K in Barcelona.
1993	Eritrea gained independence.
1995	Founding of the Federal Democratic Republic of Ethiopia under Prime Minister Meles Zenawi.
2005	Parliamentary elections, which led to rioting.
2007	according to the Julian calendar, the new millennium started in Ethiopia.

5 From Marathon to "Marathon"

Moving up to the blue ribbon event

It was inevitable. Athens proved to Haile Gebrselassie that Kenenisa Bekele, the man from his own ranks, was his heir apparent over 10K. That reassured him. After that, many saw the former "Emperor" ready to abdicate. But he was not thinking of that at all. He was carrying a different scepter: "I still have one more promise to honor," he said, one that he had made to himself. So he moved up to the blue ribbon event, the Marathon. "Too old, too late?" reporters asked him. He just gave them a friendly grin. "Just look at the history of the marathon. How old was Mamo Wolde in his first Olympic victory in Mexico City? And how old am I now?"

He genuinely felt the right age for the marathon and, if you look at his race schedule, he also had also deliberately been preparing for it. Already two years before the Athens Olympics, after his 1988 debut marathon adventure in Addis Ababa, he had a second debut, this time in the London Marathon. A successful one, with a time of 2:06:35, then the best ever time for a rookie over the 26 mile 385 yard distance. The year after Athens, with the Achilles tendon operation behind him, he regained his self-confidence with a 10mile world record, which he set from pole position in the Amsterdam Marathon. The expectations were again high. Almost nobody thought that it would be remarkable for the hitherto most successful track runner ever to celebrate a victory over the marathon distance. The headlines were only interested in a world record. In actual fact, manager Hermens had made sure that everything was in place for such a sensation. But it didn't come off. The pacemakers did not stick to the planned strategy, and in the 12km solo run through the city of Amsterdam Haile had an additional opponent, the wind. So although he finished in a personal best time, the record, as the new marathon runner put it, had to be "postponed". He added: "Just wait. Although world records can be planned on paper, they don't always come off."

London Marathon, 4.14.2002
1st Khannouchi (USA) 2:05:38,
2nd Tergat (Ken) 2:05:48,
3rd Gebrselassie (Eth) 2:06:35.

Amsterdam Marathon, 10.16.2005:
1st Gebrselassie (Eth) 2:06:20.

London Marathon, 4.16.2006
1st Limo (Ken) 2:06:39, 9. Gebrselassie (Eth) 2:09:05.

It was the same story six months later in London. Again the London Marathon and again in good shape. For a long time he ran at world record pace, but on the wet streets he then cracked. The forefoot runner had not had enough time to adjust to the conditions, and rain was not really his thing. "So I slowly started to understand the pitfalls of the blue ribbon event."

He also reflected on London, with whose organizers he had signed a contract. What about Berlin?

A school at the end of the world

Education in Ethiopia:
Only about 40% of adults and 50% of children can read and write. About 68% (2007) of children go to school. In the countryside, there are still too few schools, so that the journeys are too long.
Projects like "ABC-2015" by Karl Heinz Böhm (the charity "Menschen für Menschen" (people for people) and schools built with help from Haile Gebrselassie. In 2006, construction started of the "Marathon" school in the village of Shafamu (Welkite Province) financed by German runners.

The minibus jolted over the potholed tarmac surface behind Welkite, the center of the Gurage, the fourth-largest ethnic group, renowned farmers and traders. We were making our way towards a village called Shafamu, meaning something like "growing slowly." This place, about 150 miles from the capital city, had been identified by our friend Amanuel for an idea which had inspired our first German Marathon Travel group on its trip a year earlier. Everyone wanted to do their bit to help to build a school with the means available to shorten the route through the villages. Too many Ethiopian children left school in fourth grade. We had therefore asked Amanuel, the travel agency boss from Addis Ababa, to find suitable location for our school. "It couldn't have been easier," he reported later, "but even I, as an Ethiopian, was shocked when I saw the ruined cabin in which children from Shafamu crouched on the ground to learn. No windows, no furniture, no desks, no light. It made me cry." When we told Haile Gebrselassie later about this school and a planned appeal to the German marathon runners, he made a spontaneous decision and immediately signed up.

The lane leading up to Shafamu village could not really be called surfaced. But then we stopped; the village could only be reached down paths over the pasture and meadows, although the route was really interesting. The Gurage village comprised about 450 round huts, which extended over a good 6 miles, including fields. Clean huts with an average of ten inhabitants and well-tended gardens in which chickens and sheep were running about. That made about 4,500 inhabitants. Dotted around were shrubs that here were called Enset, known as "false bananas." A staple food of this region, where tribes boil its stems, roots and leaves to a pulp or bake them into bread. Behind the gardens, the "estates" started, on which still today as it had for centuries, the land is ploughed with wooden tools.

A classroom in Shafamu at the start and one year later. There had never been furniture in the school before.

The school corresponded to Amanuel's descriptions. Four classrooms in progress, now with four blackboards on the front walls. The start of a project. All 320 children were present, plus five teachers and two pre-school teachers. Colorful flowers were handed to us, we looked into bright eyes and a bewildered headmistress asked us several times: "Why us?" The people of Shafamu made no secret that this surprise had appeared like a star that suddenly and unexpectedly fell from heaven. We talked about the next steps. Windows with glass? That would be like in the big city! School benches for the children? Who was going to make them? The major had already given some thought to which builder from his village could oversee the building of the school. He finally put it to the vote, as the worthiest had to be nominated. He introduced us to the winner, Murga Arega, a determined, wiry man with friendly eyes.

Before we said goodbye, we started, along with the huge group of kids in the first race of their lives. A German sports good manufacturer from Havelland had given us 350 orange t-shirts, which we now distributed. The teachers understandably had a hard job keeping the kids in line. Even though for most the shirts were one size too big, it was not a problem. They were worn like jackets. Then we ran, led by an enthusiastic fellow tourist

The Marathon School – made possible by donations from German running fans in the village of Shafamu in the region of Welkite.

from Vienna, together twice around the future school, which was to be called "Marathon."

"Amanuel," I told him on behalf of the small German running group, "this is the right place. Let's continue here." And I thought as I looked back from the jolting vehicle: If there hadn't been a horizon there, I would have thought we were at the end of the world.

Haile and his first bear

It was between Welkite and Woliso when we were still in the middle of the province, that my cell phone rang. It was Berlin. What's up, anything special? Actually there was. In the middle of deepest Gurage country, I received some news that I had to have repeated. Some almost sensationally encouraging news: Haile was going to run in the Berlin Marathon, and we were going to visit him in Addis Ababa! Applause and cheers in our minibus. We would now be the first German runners to congratulate him and be able to ask him questions about it. As we got nearer to Haile's house, the driver put his foot down and had to be asked by us several times to drive more slowly. The herds of donkeys and lambs on the Ethiopian country lanes made no allowances for running tourists in a hurry.

Already on our first visit, we had tried to encourage the marathon rookie to try the flat Berlin course, where it would be possible to run fast and set records. Paul Tergat had proved it. But Haile would not give anything away though. London will have had something to do with it, and possibly also Amsterdam. Haile is not the type to commit himself, at least, not publicly. Over the years he has become as wily as a fox, who only catches the goose when he knows how to outwit it. But now he had decided on the right way to cook it!

We had arranged to meet him in the Olympic Café, and had agreed on the time by cell phone beforehand, but Haile was not there. "Have a look in the yard,"

suggested the car park attendant who watched everybody attentively from the Alem office block. Indeed, there was Haile, with a couple of employees next to an empty skip that together they were pushing on its side. The new star of the Berlin Marathon was right in the middle of the action, only distinguishable by his tracksuit. When he saw us, he waved happily and wiped the dirt off his hands. Then he greeted us, the German and Austrian guests, and invited us into his cafeteria. I already knew what would happen next: photos, autographs, questions. And always answers, even if they were difficult. He did not want to dwell on the London Marathon defeat. "I was angry about it, but now I've moved on." By which he meant his Marathon career. He had run 300 km in the previous week's training. Didn't this put a strain on the collective training with the national squad? "No way, firstly because I enjoy myself with many friends, and secondly I always run in front anyway."

Running groups went to Ethiopia between the years of 2005 and 2007.

HAILE GEBRSELASSIE

The first running tours to Ethiopia have been organized since 2005 by the travel agency Reisezeit (Berlin), including to the Abebe Bikila Marathon and the Great Ethiopian Run. These trips also include excursions to the green south and the historic north. The historic route. Lalibela: 11 rock-hewn churches and chapels are arranged in a labyrinth of stone caves, tunnels and caverns. Also known as the eighth wonder of the world. Axum: innumerable steles and monoliths can be admired here.

But he had questions too. Who were his guests? Next to him, for example, sat Eike, in his early sixties. He had already been to Ethiopia as a student, on a trek through Africa in the 1960s. Haile was amazed. Even more so when he learned of this man's current story; he was fighting cancer by running marathons, albeit in four or five hours. "After every marathon, I know that I am alive", said Eike, who had now also explored Ethiopia in the company of Berliners.

When Haile becomes serious, two furrows usually appear on his brow and his laugh is silent for a moment. There are many marathon records, not just those that can be measured with a stopwatch.

Marianne had a surprise up her sleeve that was admirably suited to the upcoming Berlin Marathon debut. She handed him a large teddy bear (the heraldic animal of the capital), to the applause of all the café guests. "This should bring you luck!" Haile beamed and as we said goodbye, he recommended that we visit the North of Ethiopia, a land full of history.

What he did not know was that the so-called Historic Route was part of the Ethiopian Tour that we had planned for two days later. After once again running behind the more than 500 Africans in the Abebe Bikila Marathon in the indomitable downtown traffic, most of the trip members were flying up in the small Fokker plane towards Gondar, Lalibela and Axum. It was both an experience and an adventure. We climbed through eleven rock churches in Lalibela, which seven hundred years ago were hewn from the red tuff for protection from enemies. Most of them, adorned with elaborate paintings and decorations, are still open for Orthodox ceremonies today. In front of the church though was something strange: emaciated human bodies, which, in line with an ancient tradition, were awaiting their last

The Royal Palace in Gondar

The Historic Route:

Lalibela: 11 rock-hewn churches and chapels are linked by a labyrinth of grottos, tunnels and caves. Also called the "eighth wonder of the world."
Axum is considered the religious capital of Ethiopia. The Ark of the Covenant is said to be located here.
Gondar: Royal City in the 17th and 18th Centuries with many palaces belonging to the then Emperors.
Bahir Da: City on Lake Tana with islands on which churches and monasteries can be found. Near the city, the source of the Blue Nile with impressive waterfalls 440 yards wide and 150 feet deep.

hours. In the royal city of Gondar, we roamed around the Gemp, the former Palace district, whose buildings resembled medieval castles. In the evening, we clinked glasses of Tedj, the local honey wine. Axum, the oldest city in Ethiopia, almost on the border with Eritrea, was said to be the resting place of the Ark of the Covenant containing the Ten Commandments, of which only a small part was visible. We were more impressed by the obelisks, much higher than those of the pharaohs in the Temple of Karnak at Luxor. They had still not all been put upright again, apparently mainly due to a lack of money. We therefore admired a great many stele that were still lying on the ground or even broken up in residents' gardens. Insights into one of the most historically rich countries in the world, with its myths, sagas and fascinating sites. And everywhere in this high altitude country, many were surprised to see greenery instead of the expected arid earth.

The field of steles in Axum. Steles look like obelisks and are the gravestones of important people.

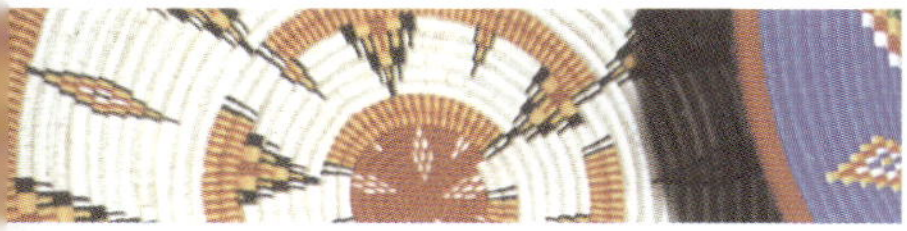

Images from the north (left) and the south of the country

The hare in the airplane

Haile was already expected in Berlin in August, long before the Berlin Marathon race. The organizers set up a press conference for Haile's debut and flew him in. The date was chosen so that the high-profile rookie could travel to Berlin after a 10km race in Palermo. The only problem was that Haile never arrived in Sicily. "The problem was" reported the four-time 10K world champion, "that during take-off, a hare was found in the engine. The pilot decided to turn back. So I was forced to miss my preparatory race for Berlin."

The rock church Bete Gyorgis.

On the sidelines of the press conference, at which he was as always relaxed, very friendly and patient, he told what some considered to be a typical Haile anecdote: "We had already been in the air for an hour and a half when it stank. We thought that lunch was ready. But it was the hare." The story reminds me of a Haile answer to the perennial question as to why he holds his left arm up when running: "As a schoolkid, I always held my school books close to my body. But don't you see that my arms now look the same? And do you know why? Because of all the autographs I have signed over the year."

Of course, this overcrowded press conference had been called to discuss Haile Gebrselassie's first Berlin Marathon appearance. Race director Mark Milde, who translated the guest's English into German, highlighted several times the organizers' joy that Haile would be competing in the 33rd running of the race. So, would there be a world record? Haile replied: "I know that I can break my friend Paul Tergat's world record, I just don't know when. Record times are run, not talked about."

When I was eating soup at the bar with Haile afterwards, I asked about the plush bear. Had he packed it in his case for luck? Haile laughed: "It has been in my trophy cabinet for a long time."

You have to know that Haile only puts items in there that commemorate victories…

So…

A windy debut: first Berlin Marathon

With the press pack through the Berlin Marathon trade fair.

He is used to press conferences, enjoys them and takes them in his stride. Two days before his first Berlin Marathon, another one was scheduled, in the radio and TV building in Masurenallee. No news was expected; he was glad that Kenyan Sammy Korir would also be running. Sammy, winner of the Rotterdam Marathon in the second best time ever. Photos were taken, short interviews and quotes, then it was over. Coach Yilma Berta consulted with Haile, for we had also invited him to a short visit of the Marathon trade fair opposite. There, our running holiday stand occupied several square feet, authorized free of charge by the organizers, SCC Running. We had displayed large photos of our joint "Marathon School" project in the village of Shafamu and the start of its construction, and appealed for donations. Among a crowd of reporters, friends and the curious he suddenly appeared at the Travel and Ethiopia stand where he thanked his fellow campaigners for their hard work. Then the caravan moved on inexorably to the Adidas zone. Sponsors take precedence after all.

HAILE GEBRSELASSIE

33rd real, Berlin Marathon, September 24th, sunny, up to 77°F

Anyone watching the marathon man from Addis Ababa warm up near the start between the Brandenburg Gate and the Victory Column, would barely have noticed any of the nervousness that is usually inevitable before any high-level race. Haile Gebrselassie had taught himself a certain self-control that also suited his character, in more than one decade to show to friends and fans. Maybe it was just a way of hiding his pre-race nerves, but he was still approaching spectators at the barriers and signing autographs. Then he lined up in pole position with the word HAILE on his running vest.

Berlin Marathon:
With more than 35,000 participants, one of the world's biggest marathon events. The first Berlin Marathon started from Grunewald on October 13th 1974 (244 finishers), in 1981, it was first held as a city marathon (2,583 finishers). In 1990, the course went through the Brandenburg Gate for the first time (22,861 finishers). In 2003, Paul Tergat ran a world record (2:04:55).

While more than 30,000 runners were still trying to take their first steps after the starting signal, at the front, the race against time had already

On the way to a first Berlin Marathon victory.

started, actually against world record pace. The Ethiopian had chosen his own pacemakers; two from his training squad, two from among the Kenyans. Stuck to his side was Sammy Korir, who had only just been beaten in Paul Tergat's Berlin world record race three years

Earlier. At first, everything went to plan. At the halfway point, Haile had the world record in his sights, even though his two pacemakers had long since dropped out. Even after 25 and 35km, he was still keeping Paul Tergat's world record pace. But then the other paid pacemakers left him in the lurch. They dropped out one after the other, and when Korir also gave up due to muscle cramps, the wonder runner raced on alone behind the leading escort vehicle. More than half an hour into the wind, which reduced his cushion of seconds yard by yard. Leipziger Strasse will stay in the lone fighter's memory for the wrong reasons. The wind blew in from all directions. The thousands on the sidewalks knew of his struggle and cheered him on. An uninterrupted wave of sympathy and encouragement flowed. At kilometer 39, he had a 12-second deficit. He just needed 61 seconds for a world record.

However, Haile Gebrselassie is a deservedly lucky man. In his famous, beaming victory pose, with both long index fingers pointing to the sky, he crossed the marathon finishing line. 2:05:56 was the best time in the world that year, and the prize money was added to his appearance money. Gete Wami, once three-time Olympic medallist on the track, was also invincible as the fastest woman, thus allowing two Ethiopian successes in Berlin to be celebrated. At the time of the victory ceremony, almost 30,000 casual runners were still on the course, to whom Haile bowed respectfully.

The following day I visited Haile in the athletes' hotel just after sunrise in order to congratulate him, which I had not been able to do in the victory hoop-la the previous day. Actually, we had agreed in Addis Ababa to meet on the Monday to go on a sightseeing tour of Berlin. Although Haile often traveled to Berlin, he only saw his hotel, training in the forest and one of the stadia. When I discovered him in the breakfast room, he had already had his plate piled high with scrambled eggs and potatoes. "There is nothing left. Sorry, hopefully more later." He was still enjoying the congratulatory wishes, signed autographs for a few waiters as they passed by and disappeared in the car of a television station.

33rd Berlin Marathon, 9.24.2006:
1st Haile Gebrselassie (Eth), 2:05:56,
2nd Gudisa Shertema (Eth) 2:10:43,
3rd Kurao Umeki (Jap) 2:13:43.
Women:
1st Gete Wami (Eth) 2:21:34,
2nd Salina Kosgei (Ken) 2:23:22,
3rd Monica Drybulska (Pol) 2:30:12.

Opening of the school with a village party.

Back in Addis Ababa, back in Shafamu

Amanuel had invited me. The school furniture was ready, made by hand, and the children and teachers were already excited. We absolutely had to visit our "Marathon school". So, another night flight to Ethiopia. Joyful reunion, no long stopover in Addis Ababa but straight on to Welkite, where, without asking much, young craftsmen had made school benches and desks out of wood in packs of three, according to pictures that we had shown them. A total of 120 pieces of furniture for the classrooms. They would now be loaded onto two trucks and prepared for the trip to the village of Shafamu the next morning. Two teachers watched carefully over the important cargo.

The inauguration of the Marathon School in the village of Shafamu on 06.09.2007. In a large-scale initiative, a German running tour group transported 310 school backpacks to Ethiopia. They were mainly collected and bought in Saxony-Anhalt and Mecklenburg-Western Pomerania, Germany.

Their arrival turned into a very emotional occasion. As the two aging trucks had different drive qualities, one jolted along with faster in front. Cheering from the 300 children, who were perfectly lined up in front of the low school buildings. None of them had ever seen such a marvel. They had all assumed it was natural to squat on the ground or sit on tree trunks in the classrooms. The load of the first truck was sufficient for two classrooms. As for the other one, it was a long story. One hour later, the second truck arrived at Marathon School, where a few quickly wiped the tears from their faces.

Now the children could learn on proper furniture, Amanuel drew my attention to a group of elderly men who were squatting in the shade of a shack. It was the Council of Elders, and they were keen to speak with us. I will never forget the meeting that followed as long as I live. Around two dozen venerable old men stood up, held out their hands and one of them, probably elected, gave a short speech, a summary of which Amanuel translated as follows: The village elders thank us, they are pleased with what we are doing for their children and grandchildren, they wish us health and a long life. Then they blessed us, according to an ancient Gurage ritual, which involved them muttering and holding out their hands to us as though they were begging.

Opening of the 'Marathon' School in the village of Shafamu on 7.9.2007.

Some days later, we met Haile and informed him of the progress of the Marathon School, and also of the donations at home. Many runners had responded to our appeal. In Parchim, Mecklenburg, North-East Germany, children had placed a piggy Bank in a bank and collected second-hand school bags in good condition. A marathon runner from Desau gave his birthday presents and offered to donate money to the village school instead. People in Erfurt, in central Germany, paid one Euro more at the start of their race and gave a check to cover the annual cost for the Kindergarten teachers. In Altmark, north of Berlin, 180 school backpacks were bought with the proceeds of a solidarity bazaar. In Frankenthal, southwestern Germany, schoolkids started sponsoring orphans from Shafamu. Jeanette, now a fan of Ethiopia, and often to be seen in a green, red and yellow tracksuit, ran around the Stuttgart area.

"You are writing history," said Haile, and was touched by what had been achieved since the start of the joint initiative. "Education is a prerequisite for Ethiopia to become a rich country." In this area, Ethiopia is still in the early stages of a marathon race. It is not so much teachers that are lacking, but schools, especially on the great plains.

'Marathon' is opened

The marathon star really wanted to be present at the opening of the school, but he had to decline because of a planned trip to England; to London in fact to plan his schedule with his manager. London of all places! He did not have happy memories of the marathon in April that he finished prematurely. After the hour race in Hengelo, for the second time in his life. He had thought that his asthma, from which he had already suffered for seven years, had been cured. In London during springtime with pollen flying around everywhere, he suddenly could not breathe. "Later, a German specialist told me that I wouldn't have been able to run any further. The attack was serious, very serious." And then what? A month later, a 10K race in Hengelo, Netherlands.

Although he ran 26:52 after a long absence from the track, he only finished fifth.

Haile started thinking about the Berlin Marathon again…

After Shafamu, 26 German running tourists traveled to inaugurate the Marathon village school after two years of construction. It had now been equipped as well as the benches and desks, with lockable doors, a teachers' lounge, many boxes full of books and pens and even glass windows. It was almost unbelievable; the first windows in the Highlands village, which was still without electricity and did not even have its own watering place. Amanuel told me a story that had happened just before our visit. A young man died, and as is the custom in many Ethiopian tribes, friends and relations appeared at the house of the dead man's family. Then they all composed themselves to return to their village huts, when they passed the new school and even more than the freshly painted walls, admired the windows made of real glass. Then their sadness turned to joy and they danced and sang.

The Marathon School – made possible by donations from German running fans in the village of Shafamu in the region of Welkite.

For the school's opening, all the parents and children had dressed up in homemade clothes and scarves in the brightest colors. The whole village seemed to be on their feet. The first part of the fund-raising campaign, bordered with school gardens, could be opened after a formal ceremony with games and singing. The guests from far-off Germany, of which most children in the village had never heard until now, had collected 310 school backpacks in a massive operation, shipped them in 21 crates and brought them from several cities

to Frankfurt and from there, largely traveling without luggage themselves to do so, to Addis Ababa and then further into deepest Ethiopia. The unbounded joy of the Shafamu children, who had never before seen such miracle bags, was the best thank you for those dedicated "whites." This June party ended with a game of soccer played between Shafamu and the tourists (2:1) and a mini-marathon (in which backpacks stayed on backs) around the new school. Almost, because all the guests were shown into a round hut where, as traditionally eaten in Ethiopia, a cooked lamb served with spicy sauces. To be eaten, of course, not with cutlery, but with the hands and torn-off pieces of injera bread.

The headmistress and mayor bode us goodbye with warm words and specially made wickerwork. Songs were also sung, by both parties. We sang "High on the Yellow Wagon" and The Rennsteig Song. The Ethiopians sang their traditional folk songs. Everyone enjoyed the other party's songs, as the applause showed, even though they had not been translated.

Cash donations for the Marathon School came from many parts of Germany. For example, from Erfurt a check raised by every starter paying an extra Euro to enter their race.

A special kind of Marathon start. The construction was progressing more and more. Haile Gebrselassie, venerated by everyone here, but hitherto only seen in newspaper photos, will travel to Shafamu one fine day.

Perhaps the village will one day produce running talent of its own?

The idea for Nazareth

Nazareth has a Derartu Tulu Boulevard.

The Abebe Bikila Marathon 2007 was to be our last. This show for the successors of Tulu, Wami, Bekele or Gebrselassie is not able to cater to casual runners from all over the world. The top coaches are looking out for top runners, which is understandable in the land of running. Due to the lack of other racing opportunities in Ethiopia, we had tried three times to sign up for the race, but without success. It is almost impossible for a central European to keep up with the hordes of several hundred Africans with times well under 3 hours, at an altitude of 8,500 feet. The traffic of the capital with its exhaust fumes was the icing on the cake. We therefore decided to run just one lap through Addis Ababa, i.e. a half marathon. Except for Gabriele from Siegen, who had proudly announced to her local newspaper that she would run a marathon in Ethiopia. For a good cause; in a unique gesture, the bakery worker had collected 3,500 euro for the school in Shafamu.

And the 52-year-old kept her word. Escorted and looked after by a vehicle belonging to our local travel agency, she reached the finishing line in the downtown stadium in 4 hours, 38 minutes. However, the otherwise so encouraging spectators fell silent when Gabriele appeared on the tartan track. She only found out why afterwards. Exactly at this time, a ceremony had started in which the opening prayer was being celebrated. We were not allowed to cheer either. We hugged Gabi without a word.

Nazareth, also called Nazret or Adama: situated about 60 miles south of Addis Ababa. Popular due to its hot springs. Green trading center, about 300,000 inhabitants. Papaya and citrus fruit plantations. Starting point for the Awash National Park.

I had spoken to Haile about the problem. It would be good for the image of the land of world class runners to hold its own international marathon. Tourism would also benefit. As impressive as the Great Ethiopian Run is with its many Ethiopian participants, no European or overseas runner would fly all the way to

Ethiopia just for a 10km race. "Make a suggestion," replied Haile, "and send it to me." So I did. Dr. Yilma Berta and friend Amanuel eventually agreed on the idea to also hold a half marathon and a 10km race as well as a marathon.

After the 2007 Abebe Bilika race, we were now following up on an idea of Yilma's: still a marathon in Ethiopia, but this time not in the capital but in Nazareth, without all the unfiltered exhaust fumes.

A little under 60 miles to the south of Addis Ababa, off the heavily trafficked highway to Kenya, lies the city of Nazareth. The city's former name was Adama, but it was renamed for the Biblical Nazareth during the time of the conversion to Christianity. The large Oromo ethnic group that occupies this area still uses the original name. "We should," the marathon coach thought out loud in the car that was taking us to Nazareth "call a future international race the Ethiopia Adama Marathon. This will immediately give the event a greater resonance in the region."

The journey to Nazareth proved to be a short one. Yilma told us about his national team that, inconceivably for us, consisted of 20 marathon men and women with personal best times that central Europeans could only envy. Amanuel gave me snippets of information about the area from time to time, especially Debre Zeit, formerly Bishoftu, a special place for many reasons. The city was teeming with vegetation, which was not surprising as it is surrounded by five crater lakes and two reservoirs that were full of flamingos, pelicans, cormorants and storks. I admired a safari lodge that not only fitted in perfectly into the landscape from an architectural point of view, but whose hut-shaped bungalows were even equipped with a spa. As we passed the gates with the monuments of former Mig Jetfighter, pilot Amanuel told us about the "cradle of the Ethiopian airforce" and its father, having served here under Emperor Haile Selassie then under Mengistu Mariam, in the 1990s was temporarily imprisoned then rehabilitated and is now retired.

Before Debre Zeit, in Dukam, Yilma talked us into taking a rest. It was to be a surprise. At the edge of the highway, Worku Bikila welcomed us to the tavern that he had set up with his prize money. It was a small hotel-restaurant with a sunny terrace, a dining area that mainly offered local dishes, of which here too Injera with Kitfo was the most requested. Out of the few photos that hung on the walls, one in particular stood out. A framed photo on which Worku Bikila was running in front of Haile Gebrselassie. A scene from the 5K World Championships in Stuttgart, Germany, where, as so often, he had selflessly supported his friend Haile Gebrselassie in pacemaking and race strategy. He finished fourth in that race.

Guests of Worku Bikila (right)

Worku was delighted at our visit, particularly at the unexpected reunion with Yilma Berta, whom he referred to as his track father. He gave us the best table in the sunniest corner of his garden, instructed his cook to grill only the finest pieces of beef and to garnish them with the best and spiciest sauces which we drank with a cool beer. We talked about the past and the future. For example, when Worku participated in Haile's world record in Hengelo, then also in his move up to the marathon. He thought that our idea of setting up an independent international run in Nazareth was terrific. "Just don't forget to stop off at my restaurant," he said.

Worku Bikila:
world class 5K and 10K runner for many years. Fourth over 5K in the 1993 World Championships in Stuttgart. Supported Haile Gebrselassie as pace maker in world record races and in his debut London Marathon in 2002. Now runs a small restaurant-hotel in Dukam, south of Addis Ababa.

Nazareth, Adama. A major city, which we first realized when we tried to find two half marathon courses. There is a boulevard a couple of miles long that leads to the towering palace of the regional government. Big stores, hotels, markets and a central square with a gyratory system, on which a gigantic poster of the first female African Olympic champion Derartu Tulu stands, for whom the main street is named. She, like many other track and field heroes, grew up and was discovered in the Arsi Province, has invested part of her prize money here, in a school for example. Nazareth has established itself as a commercial and agricultural center. The mayor is proud of his city and probably also a little because we chose it for a marathon. We would have his help to make the whole city a traffic-free zone. "For how long?" he wanted to know. About five hours, we thought. He laughed: "No problem, even seven!"

The streets are wide, usually paved in the center and really clear. They are lined with pepper trees, flame trees and bougainvillea. The doctor very quickly identified a course and seemed satisfied. He would really do all he could in the coming years to bring marathon tourists from as many countries around the world as possible.

In the Awash National Park.

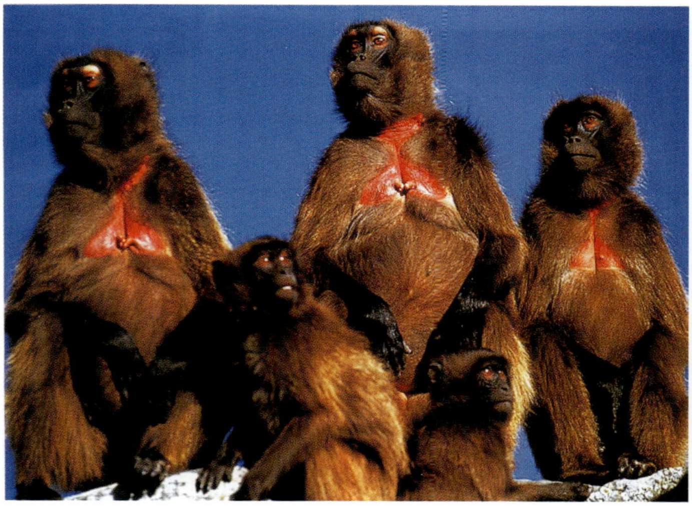

Anyone who stays in Nazareth should not forget to allow a day to visit the Awash National Park. In any case, I used my chance to travel the 60 miles there. There was not too much traffic on the road, which ran parallel to Ethiopia's only railway line to Djibouti. However, it is not usable though during the rainy season when the water washes away the track bed. The landscape changes completely. I immediately noticed that I was no longer over 5,000 feet above sea level, but descending into the western lowlands. The temperatures rose to 86°F (30°C) and even higher. Camel caravans and herds of antelopes trailed across the steppe, and suddenly, even lava fields appeared. At the wooden gate of the Awash Park, an armed guide got into our SUV, a precautionary measure more because of the current hostilities between two tribes than because of the wild animals. The National Park, the oldest and best developed in Ethiopia, is not only spectacular because of crocodiles, antelopes, gazelles and monkeys, which, if you look out for them, occasionally appear. I was particularly fascinated by the 6,500 feet high Fentale Volcano, and also the hot springs and the thundering waterfalls. But my breath was really taken away when I saw the 1,300 to 1,650 feet deep gorge of the river Awash. It reminded me of the Great Rift Valley that divides Ethiopia into two.

The Awash National Park:
A World Heritage Natural Site 55 miles east of Nazareth at an average altitude of 2,950 feet, covering 2,800 square feet, with an extinct volcano and hot springs, gazelles, gemsbuck and waterbuck, baboons, klipspringer, crocodiles, lions, 300 different types of bird. Well constructed trails.

The lion behind the small but carefully designed park museum was no longer able to strike fear into anybody. He was awkward, once lost by his mother, captured by park wardens and locked in a cage that is only opened in the evenings every now and then, so that he can pay a visit to a wild lioness.

Millennium in September

Another Haile film was made, this time by CNN during the millennium celebrations in Ethiopia. The New Year does not start here until September 12th, and while in our calendar we had already reached the year 2007, here celebrations for the change of millennium were only now being prepared.

We met fortuitously on the roof of the Alem Building. I had received an invitation to this unique millennium festival and had once again flown to Addis Ababa, taking my granddaughter, who had just sat her Abitur (final school exam). She is an adventurous jogger and had long wanted to visit the legendary country on the horn of Africa, which at the time of the Pharoahs was called Punt, later Abyssinia, and now Ethiopia, and of course if possible the legendary wonder-runner and national icon Haile Gebrselassie. I had visited the latter several times now; the easiest route was via the car park attendant of the double tower block. "Haile is up there," he said in return for a gratuity, meaning his office on the top floor. Now we just had to get past the personal assistant, but I knew her already. Haile appeared and hugged us, he held my granddaughter very close and led us up to the roof terrace, where the CNN film crew was standing in a neat row, with Hermens Junior (who had now taken over management of Haile from father Jos) right in the middle. A group photo was then taken against the majestic background of the green part of the city.

Millennium celebrations at the Gebrselassie's house.

"Revealed" was to be the name of the film production that was to star Haile Gebrselassie with whom the Americans traveled to the places where he had first learned to run, i.e. to the Arsi Highlands, and the round huts of his home village and to the school of Asela, then to the Entoto Hills, a conversation with coach Yilma Berta, interviews with reporters and finally a visit to the Gebrselassie family's private home. The celebrations of the new millennium in Addis Ababa were right on cue for the filming. Haile went along with it wonderfully, taking everything in his stride as always. Only on the actual night of 09/11 did he shun all publicity and therefore also the camera crew. So the TV people just filmed the millennium with Haile in advance. The whole Haile family (six in total) was dressed in traditional Amharic attire. Haile in a white tunic with champagne-colored scarves; the girls in bright blue clothes. They danced and sang too at the nocturnal millennium celebrations. Then though, Haile wanted some privacy. "New Year is family celebration," he said, and he also missed the official show, for which an enormous hall had been built on the Bole Road for 20,000 guests from Ethiopia, the rest of Africa and overseas.

On the roof of the Alem Building with Haile: Hermens junior, CNN film crew, the author with his granddaughter and travel organizer Amanuel.

I admit that I find the Ethiopian calendar confusing. It is the only one of its kind in the world. Only in Ethiopia do they use the Julian calendar, also called the Ethiopic Calendar. It has 13 months, 12 of which have 30 days, while the 13th is made up of the rest (5 or 6). There is also a daily 6-hour difference from central European time. It is a way of measuring time that was only introduced after the birth of Christ, according to which the new millennium, the year 2000, began on September 12th, 2007 at 12noon precisely. So we could all go to sleep, then celebrate the following day, in my opinion to slaughter another sheep and drink a beer. This was not quite how it worked out!

Millenium:
the year 2000 did not start in Ethiopia until September 12th 2007. Ethiopia is the only country in the world that still uses the Julian calendar. One year has 13 months, of which 12 have 30 days. The 13th month (Quaggimi) is very short, with only 5 or 6 days.

At night, the millennium fire burns and on New Year's morning, the children gather together.

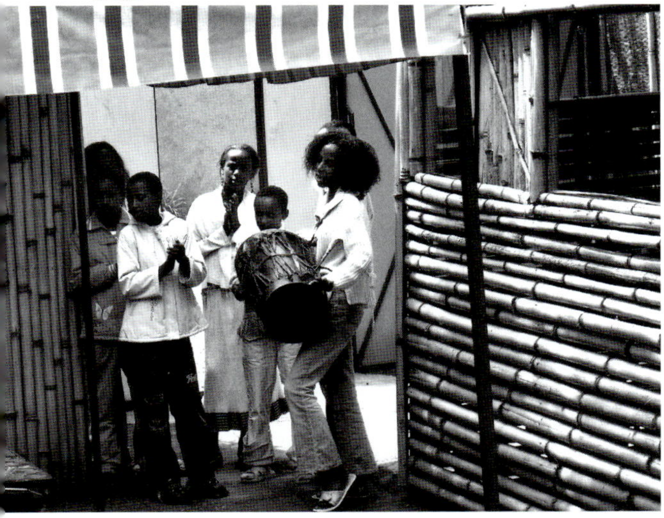

Jenny and I were invited to Mesy's house. Mesy, actually Meseret, had long black hair and big dark eyes. She works in Amanuel's travel agency and would like to specialize in marathon tours. Would we mind coming to a suburb of Addis Ababa to celebrate where the paved roads end and there are hardly any streetlamps? Mesy had to travel to work by taxi every day, because her home was not on a bus route. That reduced her monthly budget by a good third. She is ambitious, speaks good English and is now learning German at the Goethe Institute. Part of her salary also supports her family, which is currently reduced in numbers. Her mother works in the Emirates, in Dubai, as a maid, and her father works in construction, and no longer lives with her. The slender, vivacious girl therefore lives with her brother, two uncles, two aunts and a niece in two and a half rooms at the edge of the sprawling city. The hut has always been the home of her parents and grandparents.

Tesfaye, our trusty driver, had left his family because of us, and drives us to Mesy's hut where we find clean rooms, a small veranda, television, couch, armchair, chest of drawers. We are greeted very warmly and feel welcome right away. This was the first time that foreigners from far-off Germany had come down their narrow street, without being put off by the darkness and puddles of water. Dark, curious eyes peered from the neighboring huts. We are asked to sit on the best armchairs, while the curtain to the next room keeps opening to reveal an uncle or aunt wishing us "Endemn ameshu", good evening. Of course, they want to check out Mesy's visitors.

The television set is on all the time on this September 11th evening, only interrupted by the usual brief power outages. The government's gala event was broadcast live, everyone listens carefully, reacts to speeches, shows their surprise vociferously, when the Prime Minister in traditional costume appears, enjoying with us the singing and dancing in the diversity of the multi-ethnic multitude of this their beautiful country.

The symbol of the Ethiopian Millennium Festival: a coffee bean in a green yellow and red flag.

Meanwhile, an aunt seated on a low stool is roasting coffee beans in an elaborate ceremony that we are asked to sniff and which then, after our approval, are processed into a delicious Ethiopian espresso. But first there is "local beer," home-brewed, full-flavored and quite low in alcohol. The flat bread dish with plenty of meat, vegetables and sauces was now ready and was arranged nicely in a round basket. We are handed bowls of water in which to wash our hands. Jenny was slightly bewildered when the best morsels are pushed into our mouths by Mesy, which is a special honor.

Around two hours before midnight, we are asked to go out onto the street, where a fire is prepared. Everyone receives a huge bundle of sticks that they light on the fire. As guests, we have to blow the first rising smoke in Mesy's home, which is said to bring luck for the year to come. Then we all dance without stopping and sing loudly around the first crackling, then blazing fire. Of course, we don't understand a single word, only when the groups of neighboring kids sing "Haile, Haile" do we ask why. "They are improvising," explains Mesy, "and all the names they know appear in their songs." Haile is just the most famous of them.

Tesfaye drives us into the city an hour before midnight. Today it takes a long time. From all around, people are streaming in their hundreds and thousands to Meskel Square. They are dressed up, holding green, yellow and red millennium flags in their hands, singing and shouting greetings to each other. Many are holding their beer glasses in their hands, probably to clink glasses. Hardly anybody can afford any other alcoholic drinks. We halt at one of the downtown tower blocks, the Milk House. Here there a just a couple of free places in the top floor, but instead of milk, beer or wine are being served.

Below us lies Addis Ababa at night, which is about to be illuminated by a colorful fireworks display. At midnight, the advent of the new millennium is greeted with loud cheers.

On the morning of September 12th, when according to the ancient custom, the Ethiopian children go from house to house to collect a few Birr by singing songs, Haile Gebrselassie reads in the newspaper that he has been voted "Athlete of the Millennium."

Back on top with a world record

Haile's hunt for the world record in the endurance runners' blue ribbon event was a long one. In his Berlin Marathon debut, he nearly did it, in Fukuoka, nothing of the kind was planned, but the time still proved to be respectable. Then came the airborne pollen in London, which was a disaster for him. Haile, being the man he is, did not give up, did a series of allergy tests and prepared for Berlin again. "I knew that I would have no breathing problems in Berlin in September, on a course that suited me better than all the others." He increased his weekly mileage and worked on his finishing speed, but had to expect that he would have to run the last part of the Marathon alone against himself and the clock.

Haile Gebrselassie was elected Ethiopia's "athlete of the millennium". In a poll for the "businessman of the millennium", he finished 3rd.

Two test runs eventually gave him the certainty that he would be able to achieve his aim. In Ostrava, at the Golden Spikes meet, he ran the equivalent of two world records in a 20km race, during which he lowered the world record for the one hour run. He completed the New York half marathon in first place in under an hour, commenting that the hills of Central Park had hurt his final time.

Before the 2007 Berlin Marathon, the media was invited to two press conferences with Haile. At the first, again organized in August, the subject of all the questions was on the world record of his friend and eternal rival Paul Tergat. Haile was used to this, and again and again avoided answering, instead referred to September 30th, when everything must be right: wind and temperature, pace makers and rivals, and not least his own form. Was it the sponsors who were pushing him to clock a certain time? Haile took it in his stride, although he knew that it would be hard for him to achieve this time. He would be happy to beat Paul Tergat's time. But as requested, he sketched a running stick figure and underneath it the time of 2:03:00 and added: "It is possible, but when?"

At the press conference at the 2007 Berlin Marathon Haile sketched his marathon record wish.

The organizers held the second press conference two days before the race as usual. A beaming star immediately won the hearts of the media, but was no longer so open about the world record attempt, which could also be picked up from his sparkling eyes in his dark face, and after the statements was available for reporters. Towards the end of the conference, I pushed myself forward as well, for I had a special mission to perform: one of our Marathon school donors had given me one of the famous, colorful ceramic bears and asked me to be sure to pass it on to Haile before the start. He remembered that the previous year, we had presented him with a stuffed bear, now the second bear would also bring him luck. Haile laughed; of course he knew about and liked the history of the bear. I quickly documented the event on the sidelines with a photo.

Then the time had come. On Saturday, he had looked out of the hotel window in a state of shock, laughing no longer, because outside the rain did not let up. Then he seriously wondered whether he was in the right place. However, Sunday morning was perfect. Haile beamed like the sun and before the start, again went up to his fans.

He was given a special vest number by race director Mark Milde.

HAILE GEBRSELASSIE

34th real,-Berlin Marathon, September 30th 2007, 59 – 63°F (15 - 17°C):

Right from the start of the race he asserts himself as favorite from the more than 33,000 participants, accompanied by five pace makers, who also protect him like bodyguards. The conditions are almost windless and the temperature good for running. He reels off the kilometers like a well-oiled machine, completing the first 20 kilometers between 2:54 and (just once) 3:00 minutes. His half marathon time is 62:29, eighteen seconds faster than the previous year. The spectators realize what is happening and don't stop cheering him on. Later, Haile said that it seemed to him as though this time there were twice as many spectators along the course. At kilometer 30, when the last two pacemakers finally drop out, he is 29 seconds up on Paul Tergat's world record pace. He thanks fellow countryman Eshetu Wondimu and Kenyan Rogers Bob with a thumbs up and heads off alone towards the Brandenburg Gate. The final kilometer times without competition are almost all covered in 2:52 minutes. What a pace!

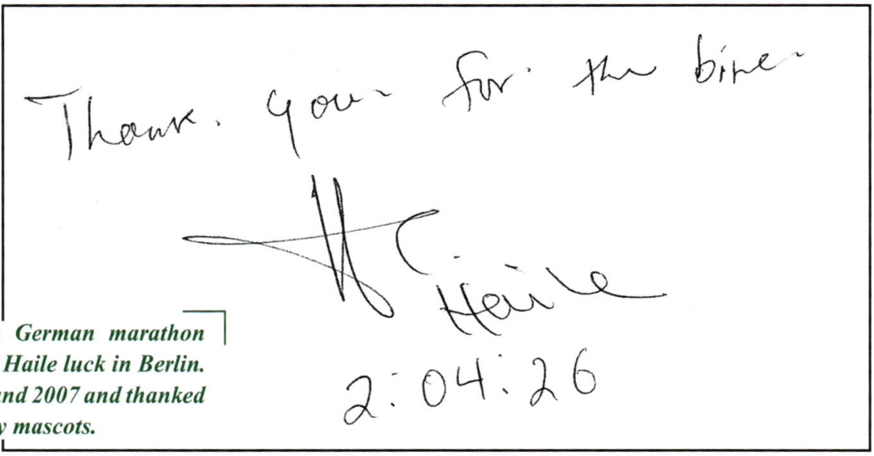

Two bears from German marathon runners brought Haile luck in Berlin. He won in 2006 and 2007 and thanked us for these lucky mascots.

A speed of 20:35km per hour is reached at the finish, when the new world record holder crosses the line in 2:04:26, apparently effortlessly, smiling broadly as usual. Again, he points both index fingers to the sky as a victory sign. The dreams of the little Ethiopian with the big heart and that of the Berlin Marathon team have come true.

34th Berlin Marathon: 9.30.2007: 1st Haile Gebrselassie (Eth) 2:04:26 – WR, 2nd Sammy Kirui (Ken) 2:06:51, 3rd Salim Kipsang (Ken) 2:07:29. Women: 1st Gete Wami (Eth) 2:23:17, 2nd Irina Mikitenko (Ger) 2:24:51, 3rd Helena Kirop (Ken) 2:26:27.

The hoopla at the finish was endless. Haile did not seem to mind; he was there for everyone anyway. He gave interviews to the reporters, blew kisses to the Berlin public, hugged Gete Wami, his teammate, as she had just made it an Ethiopian double. On the first cell phone that race director Mark Milde handed him he heard the voice of Alem and the singing of his family and friends at home. Congratulations from home just a few minutes after the finish: a new experience. For the first time, the Berlin Marathon had been broadcast live in the African Highlands; all available television sets were surrounded, not just in Addis Ababa. "You know," the wonder runner once explained to me, "Although people first say that Haile has won," then they add: "Ethiopia has won." The second phone call came from Kenya. Paul Tergat, the dethroned world-record-holder, first congratulated the race director and then his friend and now the new king of the marathon. Haile thanked him and apologized at the same time: "Sorry Paul for taking the record away from you. But you can still try to get it back."

Then came the medal presentation with laurel wreath, lap of honor to the Brandenburg Gate and back, then autographs for many arriving runners on their vest numbers. It was a happy Sunday. My attempts to get near to my now good acquaintance were at first unsuccessful. I was trying to introduce him to two marathon runners who were standing

Surrounded by his pace makers through Berlin Moabit.

in the background. One of them was the fastest German to cross the finishing line, where he was welcomed by his father: Falk, the former triathlete, trained by Waldemar Cierpinski. I knew that the two-time Olympic Marathon champion (the only one after Abebe Bikila to have pulled off this double) would love to shake Haile's hand.

At the winner's press conference, Haile headed towards me. He grinned at me across the room, hugged me and whispered in my ear: "The bear!" He had not forgotten that for the second time he had received a lucky bear from his German friends. Then he passed me a piece of paper on which he had written: "Thank you for the bear." This thank you note now hangs with the presentation photo in a Berlin office.

Haile on the way to a world record 2:04:26.

Interview after the Berlin Marathon

Plenty of questions and plenty of answers, the winner could not affirm often enough how happy he was. And it showed. Even an always smiling Haile had never looked so radiant. But what next? Would the Berlin Marathon now take a back seat? Would Beijing be an Olympic marathon triumph? Or would such dreams be dashed by the smog and high air humidity? The new king of the marathon scene asked for a break, a pause in which to reflect and reorganize. "For the time being I am happy with the world record that is now mine."

from "Laufzeit" 11/2007

Haile Gebrselassie's World Record run

km mark	km time	km split times
1 km	2:57	0:02:57
2 km	3:00	0:05:57
3 km	2:57	0:08:54
4 km	2:56	0:11:50
5 km	2:53	0:14:43
6 km	2:55	0:17:38
7 km	2:59	0:20:37
8 km	2:54	0:23:31
9 km	2:56	0:26:27
10 km	2:57	0:29:24
11 km	2:58	0:32:22
12 km	2:58	0:35:20
13 km	2:58	0:38:18
14 km	2:58	0:41:16
15 km	2:58	0:44:14
16 km	2:59	0:47:13
17 km	2:58	0:50:11
18 km	2:59	0:53:10
19 km	2:59	0:56:09
20 km	2:59	0:59:08
21 km	3:00	1:02:08
22 km	2:58	1:05:06
23 km	3:01	1:08:07
24 km	2:58	1:11:05
25 km	2:59	1:14:04
26 km	2:59	1:17:03
27 km	3:00	1:20:03
28 km	2:59	1:23:02
29 km	2:52	1:25:54
30 km	3:00	1:28:54
31 km	2:57	1:31:51
32 km	2:56	1:34:47
33 km*	3:00	1:37:47
34 km*	3:00	1:40:47
35 km	2:50	1:43:37
36 km	2:56	1:46:33
37 km	2:55	1:49:28
38 km	2:52	1:52:20
39 km	2:52	1:55:12
40 km	2:55	1:58:07
41 km	2:52	2:00:59
42,195 km	-	2:04:26
1. HM		1:02:29
HM		1:01:57
Corresponds to		2.54min/km 20.35km/hr, 5.65mph

* = estimated (33km marker was probably in the wrong place)

6 More Searching

Winter in Africa

June in Addis Ababa. Was it still African autumn or already the start of winter? Barely anybody gives any thought to whether Krempt (winter) starts exactly on June 2nd of the European month or on the 8th of the Ethiopian months, here called Senee. For after my arrival, I was told of other, much more serious concerns. In autumn, the "short rainy season" had as good as failed, with disastrous consequences. The lack of water led to shortages in the hydroelectric power plants around the capital. Every district of Addis Ababa had power cuts lasting several hours three days per week. I quickly got used to my boarding house landlord placing a few candles in my bedroom and bathroom in the evening with a typical Ethiopian smile. I was also forced to accept that the TV coverage of the European Soccer Championships would be interrupted. But what had the inhabitants of these Highlands had to put up with since my last stay! Not only energy but also food prices had risen enormously, sometimes even by a third. "Now the small middle class is already falling into poverty," moaned Andy, the travel guide from last year, whom I met. "It is now not just the homeless who are happy to have just one meal a day."

The view over Addis Ababa from Haile's office.

At the end of the month of July, everyone hoped that there would be enough electricity again.

For brief showers already heralded the arrival of the long rainy season. The air is also humid and warm at this time. In the Highlands it is bearable; in the lowlands, the temperatures soar to more than 86°F (30°C). Did you know that in the Damakil Desert, near Eritrea, temperatures of 140°F (60°C) in the shade have been recorded? It is

Haile in his office

one of the hottest regions on earth. Only when the long rainy season descends, when the rain is sometimes torrential, do people in Ethiopian talk of winter. Addis Ababa is often under water for days. At the latest in August, everyone rejoices in the spring, which starts with the New Year's festivities in September.

It is now very different on the Horn of Africa.

As I had not yet arranged to meet with Haile, I used the time for other activities. I went back to "our" school in Shafamu with my friend Amanuel. The headmistress could not be reached by cell phone. As it emerged later, she had sent the phone to Welkite, 20 miles away, to be recharged, where there were electric sockets and electricity. So the surprise was all the greater when we jolted through the village on a truck laden high with school benches. There was no holding back the children of the newly built school building and they eagerly dragged the new furniture into their classrooms by themselves. We looked around us and were really impressed. Since the opening of the school a year previously, not only had the flowers in the front yards grown colorful and high, the 3rd grade now had its own home, and the completion of the teachers' accommodation seemed to be imminent. What only 130 square feet of living space per teacher means can only be measured by someone who has experienced having to wade 2½ miles back and forth through the mud of Shafamu day after day in the rainy season.

The headmistress's room was turning into a kind of school museum. Photos, documents and souvenirs of our previous visit, even the limp remains of the colorful balloons, now decorated the walls. The round station clock, a present from runners from Stendhal, Germany, was now visible on the wall with its hands of course turned back six Ethiopian hours. I asked for a poster written by hand in Amharic to be translated for me. It listed the names on a School

Women on the roads in the Welkite region. Umbrellas, as big as possible, are essential in the rain and also in the sunny season.

Council, which met monthly and of which (as the dedicated but reserved headmistress proudly noted) a pupil was also a member. Amanuel meanwhile explored other new developments. So this elementary school named Marathon, created thanks to donations by German runners, had become a showpiece in this region, which comprises 64 villages. Everyone wants to study here, many just turn up, but the capacity of 419 girls and boys for seven classrooms is quickly exhausted.

We then came out with a final, apprehensive question: "What has happened to the German school backpacks donated last year?" We couldn't see them anywhere. Had they been sold off? Or had they even been put to practical use as a means of transport for the work in the fields? The headmistress first looked slightly irritated, then she laughed heartily: "No, no, they are under the benches, in the shelves. They are sacred to us. Nobody may enter the school without his or her bag."

In search of Gold

Where is Haile's gold medal from Atlanta? I heard that he had donated it to a church in the Entoto Hills. But which one? I set out to search for it. My search first led me to the Maryam Church, the largest and most famous on the path to the 9,800 foot peak. Early each morning, big groups of the white-robed faithful made the pilgrimage here. At the same time, the running gods climbed out of their tracksuits in the church's car park.

When I arrived the mass had already been read. There was peace in the Eucalyptus forests. Behind the Maryam Church, I climbed the wooden remains of the former palace of Menelik II, the founder of the capital city at the end of the 19th Century. It was quite a unique feeling to stand on the rickety veranda where the Imperial wife once looked in the wide valley and convinced her consort: "Menelik, let's stay here!"

There are many different religions. About 40% of Ethiopians are Orthodox Christians, 10% are Protestants, 45% Muslims. Christianity and Islam coexist peacefully. The many religious festivals include the Meskel Festival to commemorate the finding of the true Cross on September 27th, which is springtime here. There are also natural religions among certain ethnic groups

In front of the Imperial Palace, a well looked after Menelik Museum. Could the Olympic Gold of running emperor Gebrselassie be kept here? With the help of a museum warden and his torch, I actually did find a glass cabinet with shiny medals and a glass cup, also including an Olympic Gold medal, albeit that of Gezahgne Abera from Sydney. And next to it, Berhane Adere's World Championships Gold medal from Paris. The not exactly decorative but definitely huge cup belonged to Haile for his Dubai Marathon victory. Unfortunately, no gold medal from Atlanta was to be seen.

Jeepdriver Dedeje, who was driving me through Addis this time, did not need much time to think. On the other side of the Entoto Hills there was another church, the Kidame Mirete. We snaked back down into the valley, past the many dozens of textile stalls, then Dedeje abruptly changed direction and drove us back up to Entoto, confidently avoiding all the pilgrims, burden carriers and straggler rams in the process. In a forest, quite hidden away and as such far from the madding crowd of the city, the place of worship we were seeking appeared, a pretty, polygonal, wooden building. But unfortunately it was locked.

Ethiopian running stars dedicated Olympic medals to these two churches: the Maryam Church

We asked a priest about Haile's gold medal. Yes, he knew about it. It was here, but not inside the church, as it unfortunately did not have a museum, in a box that was firmly locked. Our request to see it was met with a shaken head. The man who had the key was not available then. Dedeje pointed to me and explained to the priest that I had come from Germany especially and could he not just see what he could do? He went to consult a priest and after a lengthy argument, made an unexpected suggestion: I was to find the highest Orthodox leader, the Bishop of Addis Ababa and obtain written permission. Then they would do all they could to get the box opened.

Haile's gold from Atlanta is kept in the latter in the Kidame Mirete Church.

My initial speechlessness was followed by understanding. It was now obvious how much importance was attached to Haile's first Olympic gold medal. Both for his favorite church, from which he had started hundreds of training runs and in which he had prayed a hundred times, and also for the entire, long-suffering country of Ethiopia, for whom this noble metal from Atlanta was a great consolation.

Pre-Olympic problems – what now?

At the start of January 2008 everything seemed to be in order in Haile's running world. The 34-year-old did not want to lose out on the $250,000 prize money for winning the Dubai Marathon. It would also mark a firm starting point for that Olympic year. There was also a million dollar prize for a world record. If the Sheikh of the Emirates could afford it…Haile saw the financial opportunity, won, and missed his own world best time by 28 seconds. Was he satisfied? Not quite, as his coach Dr Yilma Berta later told me. For the wonder runner had actually set his heart on winning the million dollars. "Dubai is one of the flattest marathon courses in the world," said Yilma, "and if the pacemaker had not gone off too fast at the start, a new world record would have been set." The first 10 kilometers were clocked in 28:39 minutes. The Beijing Marathon was still in Haile's sights.

On the flat marathon course in Dubai.

But this had changed by the time he smashed the world's best time of the year on the fast half marathon course along Lisbon's Tagus River. There he hinted that he would not be competing in the Olympic 26mile 285yard race. His reason: "The air pollution in China is a potential health hazard." After his experience in London, he was afraid that the Beijing smog could permanently damage his health. His withdrawal from the marathon shocked the world so much that three days later he was forced to make another statement: his decision was sports-related, not political. He was not objecting to China's hosting of the Olympics and he valued the efforts of the organizers. As an asthma sufferer, he was only concerned about his own well-being.

At the end of March, another press conference was held in which the two-time Olympic champion mentioned the possibility of running the 10K in Beijing. Then followed a statement at the start of April by the Ethiopian national coach Dr. Wolde Kostre, which made a tour of the agencies in the world: "He [Haile Gebrselassie]

Dubai Marathon, 1st18.2008:
Men
1st Haile Gebrselassie (Eth) 2:04:53 h ($250,000),
2nd Isaac Macharia (Ken) 2:07:16 h ($100,000),
3rd Sammy Korir (Ken) 2:08:16 h.

Women
1st Birhane Adere (Eth) 2:22:42 h,
2nd Bezunesh Bekele (Eth) 2:23:09 h ($100,000)
3rd Askale Tafa (Eth) 2:23:23 h ($50,000)

Lisbon Half Marathon, 3.16.2008:
1st Haile Gebrselassie (Eth) 59:15.

Hengelo 10K, 5.4.2008:
1st Sileshi Sihine (Eth) 26:50.53,
2nd Haile Gebrselassie (Eth) 26:51.20.

can no longer live with the youngsters over 10K. We have five with times under 27 minutes....we love and respect him, but he won't be able to keep up."

Emperor Gebrselassie reacted with slight annoyance. Now he wanted to show the doubters, and he did so, that as a thirty-something, he was not yet ready for the scrap heap over 10K on the track. In Hengelo, often the venue for his records, he ran a race like in the good old days: 26:50.20 – nine seconds below the Ethiopian Olympic qualifying standard, thus qualifying him for Beijing.

Beijing is good, Berlin is better...

Haile kept me waiting. As usual, he had been invited to give an annual lecture at Addis Ababa University. He let his coach know by cell phone that this time it would last a little longer. I looked through the photos in his office: Haile as a youngster, Haile as Olympic champion, Haile with his family. When he then arrived an hour late, he laughed and was still completely on a high after the previous hour in the auditorium. "500 students, I have never spoken in front of so many before. It was a fantastic atmosphere. I didn't want to leave, sorry."

Haile at his desk, often with his cell phone that is usually wedged between his ear and his shoulder. It is the only way for the selected few to contact him. Emails, normal telephone calls and mail are intercepted by his personal assistant.

I had already shown him two different covers and many pages of photos for this new book. Haile seemed keen particularly on the cover picture, and immediately got involved: "Use the photo of the Berlin Marathon and put the title in red," he suggested, then went on: "No, you are the 'owner,' you must decide yourself." So, the Berlin Marathon is booked? "I have signed the contract. I look forward to Berlin, your capital city is my favorite after my own." He looked at two photos with particular interest. One showed his parents' round hut in the village near Assela. The other held his attention for longer. At the previous year's press conference, he had drawn a stick man next to the time of 2:03. At the time, he had just grinned at it and not allowed himself to be drawn on the subject. Here on the seventh floor of the Alem Building, he now mused: "That's quite a time. I believe that in Berlin it is possible, but of course, only if all the conditions are right."

Round huts (here in the village of Shafamu), typical of those in the rest of the country. The Gebrselassies also grew up in these windowless homes.

At this, I took a small gift out of my bag and was surprised at how enthusiastically he received it. It was a mini Berlin plush bear, really nothing special, just a typical souvenir of the capital. He immediately remembered that he had been given a bear before each Berlin Marathon start, which had always (he said with his unmistakable laugh) brought him luck. Two stood in his trophy cabinet at home, the third was now entrusted to the care of son Naty, just three years old. So that he would not forget the little bear, he hid it underneath his training jacket. "Beijing is good," he said, "but Berlin is better."

Haile receives a third bear from us in his office.

So goodbye to the Beijing Marathon! But he would still be running the 10K for the fourth time in an Olympic Games and this time hopefully injury-free. However, he objected to my question as to whether his compatriots like Kenenisa Bekele or Seleshi Sihine would provide tough opposition. His brow furrowed and the Haile smile disappeared for a moment. "You know, whoever doesn't race to win has already lost."

The next guests were knocking outside. It would be his next door neighbors, whom he had invited to visit his office. Now we would hardly see each other. And the next day he had to go to Jimma right after training.

In Jimma, the coffee-growing region, a special honor awaited him. He was to receive an Honorary Doctorate from the Medical School there. The third one after Dublin and Leeds!

There was not much news, even coach Yilma Berta, otherwise always good for an email, had very little to say. I understood that Olympic preparations were taking up all his time. Even Haile was withdrawing more and more from the limelight.

The finishing medal for the real,-Berlin Marathon 2008.

For the first time in the history of this long-standing event, a medal was issued with the portrait of a world class runner who is still racing – and in this particular case had even entered the race!

Slight unrest was spreading among the Berlin Marathon organizers. Although I brought the good news that Haile had signed his contract, the contract had still not arrived. They did not get the OK from the Dutch management until July 22nd, after which they could proceed with the prepared press statement: "World record holder Haile Gebrselassie has committed to running for a third time – a great event is in store."

I admit that I was also a little worried as in the final months before the Olympics I watched Sileshi Sihine and Kenenisa Bekele grab the headlines over Haile Gebrselassie's former speciality the 10K. Sihine, when he won in Hengelo in front of his hero; Bekele, when he ran the fourth-fastest 10K of all time in the USA. Manager Jos Hermens, himself an experienced runner, now spoke in interviews to put Haile's hopes into perspective. "He will finish the 10K without a medal. He is running because he feels he owes it to his fellow Ethiopians. The whole nation wants him to run, now that he has pulled out of the Beijing Marathon."

Long-distance calm then returned; the calm before the Olympic storm in the Chinese metropolis. It started with a brilliant opening ceremony fireworks display that swept through the "birds' nest". Immediately afterwards, an Internet message flashed on my computer. Zhang Yanjun, the knowledgeable and always friendly tourist guide from Xi'an, the city of the terracotta soldiers, had sent an excited email. She had not seen Haile Gebrselassie marching with the Ethiopian Team in the opening ceremony on television. Was he still coming? She remembered that the African world record holder was also very popular in her homeland. In February he had visited Beijing to check out the weather and the marathon course. During that visit, a photo was taken that endeared Haile to this gigantic country. He was running with Chinese children and was a firm supporter of a charity campaign for needy boys and girls.

Would the Beijing Olympics go ahead without the hero of Atlanta and Sydney?

I managed to solve the mystery. Distance runners from high altitude in Africa or elsewhere fly to their competitions as late as possible. So the man of many superlatives was also preparing for his fourth Olympics, and again, a little out of necessity this time, for the 10K on the track.

August 18th, 2008, Olympic 10K, sunny, temperature around 71.5°F (22°C), 90,000 spectators in the Beijing 'Birds' Nest' Stadium

The excitement in the stands of the impressive steel stadium was first shared between the triple jump, hurdles and 10K, but then concentrated solely on the 25-lap race. The majority of the 39 runners stayed together, with no discernible tactical strategy. Eritrea's duo carried the pace for a long time at the front; the three Ethiopians Bekele, Sihine and Gebrselassie held back. Four laps before the finish, the Kenyans tried to take control of the race, Haile joined in and tried to hold back the competition from these two neighboring countrymen. As the finale approached, Kenenisa Bekele stepped up and sprinted away unstoppably, and Sileshi Sihine again fought successfully for the silver medal. Haile Gebrselassie finished sixth and was not unhappy. He embraced the new long-distance hero, who was now, like him, a double Olympic champion over this distance. All three ran together, with the green, yellow and red Ethiopian flag wrapped around them, laughing as they ran past a crowd of cheering and dancing compatriots in the stands. "That wasn't bad at all," commented Geb into the microphone. "Although I could no longer sprint over the last 300m. I just didn't have it in my

2008 Beijing Olympics, men's 10,000m:
1st Kenenisa Bekele (Eth) 27:01.17
2nd Sileshi Sihine (Eth) 27:02.77
3rd Micah Kogo (Ken) 27:04.11
4th Moses Masai (Ken) 27:04.11
5th Zersenay Tadese (Eri) 27:05.11
6th Haile Gebrselassie (Eth) 27:06.68

Kenenisa Bekele's joy at his second resounding Olympic 10,000m victory.

Beijing 2008: Ethiopian Tirunesh Dibaba was the first woman to win both the Olympic 5,000m and 10,000m.

legs. I am now a marathon runner." With his winning laugh, this time he did not refrain from making a prediction: His career was far from over. He wanted to compete internationally for at least another ten years. And as a trump card, the Olympics would be taking place in London in four years' time. Abebe Bikile was not forgotten…

"I will not be too old at 39", he says, looking the interviewer in the eye and raising both hands as if to defend himself. "Mamo Wolde was 40 in Munich at the World Championships and finished third. I still have two great ambitions: Olympic victory and a world record below 2:04." And with this, he again gave Berlin reason to cheer. The Olympic Birds' Nest was, from this point of view, a good test for the fourth Marathon at the Brandenburg Gate.

Berlin forever?

Silesi Sishine, Kenenisa Bekele and Haile Gebrselassie on the lap of honour

I am now sure that all the reporters now look forward most to the press conferences in the Marriott Hotel on the Potsdamer Platz. Sometimes, a few Ethiopian fans even manage to get past the doormen and find a seat in the conference room. Whether before or after the Berlin Marathon, they all experience a Haile who is not only always in a good mood but can also chat wittily and give clear answers to all questions. He also patiently takes the time to answer requests, make statements into microphones and sign autographs.

When Bekele won the Olympic 5,000m six days later (12:57.82), he equalled the feat of Miruts Yifter who was the first to win gold over both distances in Moscow in 1980 and carried the Ethiopian flag in the opening ceremony in Beijing.

Questions and answers: "Could you imagine being President of your country?" "Yes indeed, but first let me run a few marathons. And remember: I have a growing company in Addis where I want to create more jobs. Just let things take their course." Then, as expected, the inevitable question about a world record. Haile: "It is probably only possible here. Berlin is a wonderful city, the enthusiastic people, the ideal course, the special atmosphere. If the weather cooperates, anything is possible." "What do you think the world record time will be in coming years?" "2:02 in five years." "And on Sunday?" "Perhaps a new record."

The organizer had actually allowed me a bit of a coup in this first press conference. Haile knew about the book, but not about the present that I was about to give him: a copy of the first edition of "Der Wunderläufer – Haile Gebrselassie" (Haile Gebrselassie – the Wonder Runner). Many reporters who had been on their way to the exit turned around again. Finally there was a

The author of this book, Klaus Weidt, hands Haile the first edition.

book in German about the likeable running star. So, flash photographs and requests to include dedications in the book. It was lucky that I had brought a whole pile with me just in case.

Haile beamed of course, as he always did. He flicked through it, looked at the pictures, and commented later a little sadly that he actually could not read the book. His German was not yet good enough. Would it be possible to publish it in English? I promised him that I would do my best. Two years later, an important publisher told me that he would not only publish a second edition but also have it translated…

35th real.-Berlin Marathon, September 28th, 2008, 54 – 68°F (12 - 20°C)

Haile Gebrselassie approaches the 42.195 kilometer Berlin Marathon with total concentration from the first step. The weather suits him. The dry air and also the 54°F (12°C) at the start are similar to the usual temperatures in his native Entoto Hills at this time of year. 3:05 minutes for the first kilometer is a relatively slow pace for him and is only measured again at the thirteenth, at which point he is now on course for world-record pace with times well below three minutes. At no point in the race is Haile aware of the pains of a few weeks ago in his left calf, which were so strong that his manager Jos Hermens suggested dropping out of the Berlin Marathon. A week's rest followed, unbeknownst to all. Now it was history.

The Berlin Marathon sticker of 2008 showing Haile's victory in 2007.

The strong Kenyan, James Kwambai, is a rival who will motivate him to run at the required pace, in addition to the pacemakers. When the former is still at his side at 25 km, he tries to pile on the pressure and is surprised. "I haven't got rid of him," he said later. He only manages to shake him off after another eleven kilometers.

Already before the half marathon point, everything is pointing to a new record time. Last year he was clocked at 1:02:08 at 21km, this time it is 22 seconds quicker.

35th real.-Berlin Marathon, 9.28.2008:
1st Haile Gebrselassie (Eth) 2:03:59 – WR
2nd James Kwambai (Ken) 2:05:36,
3rd Charles Kamathi (Ken) 2:07:48

Women:
1st Irina Mikitenko (Ger) 2:19:19,
2nd Askale Magarsa (Eth) 2:21:31,
3rd Helena Kirop (Ken) 2:25:01

Even running by himself he is unstoppable, becoming gradually even quicker and finally carried along by the cheers of the multitude through the Brandenburg Gate to the finish. 2:03:59 – a new world record. The man in yellow has triumphed again. He snatches the green, yellow and red national flag and laughs and celebrates: "Yes, this is a dream come true…the spectators could not have been better, it was like being in a full stadium." And later, in front of the press in answer to the question, "what next?" he predicted: "Perhaps I can even run 2:03:30. But in principle I am running against my age."

The finish of the 35th real,-Berlin Marathon

This record result had allowed the 2008 Berlin Marathon to reach a new dimension, and it became the number one marathon in the world. At the evening winners' party, Haile was not only cheered by many thousands of fans for uttering the legendary Kennedy phrase: "Ich bin ein Berliner" (I am a Berliner), but also for this one: "I'll be back!"

I met Haile very briefly in the May of the following year, between the office and sauna of his business premises. He was delighted with further copies of our book and told me that he had been able to increase his work force even more, to a couple of hundred, some only temporary, some permanent.

Haile Gebrselassie split times		
Km Mark	time	km time
1 km	0:03:05	0:03:05
2 km	0:05:57	0:02:52
3 km	0:08:48	0:02:51
4 km	0:11:44	0:02:56
5 km	0:14:34	0:02:50
6 km	0:17:30	0:02:56
7 km	0:20:23	0:02:53
8 km	0:23:18	0:02:55
9 km	0:26:16	0:02:58
10 km	0:29:13	0:02:57
11 km	0:32:09	0:02:56
12 km	0:35:06	0:02:57
13 km	0:38:12	0:03:06
14 km	0:41:10	0:02:58
15 km	0:44:02	0:02:52
16 km	0:46:59	0:02:57
17 km	0:49:57	0:02:58
18 km	0:52:56	0:02:59
19 km	0:55:52	0:02:56
20 km	0:58:50	0:02:58
21 km	1:01:46	0:02:56
Half Marathon	1st half	2nd half
	1:02:04	1:01:55
22 km	1:04:46	0:02:42
23 km	1:07:44	0:02:58
24 km	1:10:42	0:02:58
25 km	1:13:40	0:02:58
26 km	1:16:39	0:02:59
27 km	1:19:34	0:02:55
28 km	1:22:36	0:03:02
29 km	1:25:31	0:02:55
30 km	1:28:25	0:02:54
31 km	1:31:26	0:03:01
32 km	1:34:18	0:02:52
33 km	1:37:13	0:02:55
34 km	1:40:06	0:02:53
35 km	1:43:05	0:02:59
36 km	1:46:00	0:02:55
37 km	1:48:53	0:02:53
38 km	1:51:48	0:02:55
39 km	1:54:39	0:02:51
40 km	1:57:33	0:02:54
41 km	2:00:21	0:02:48
42 km	2:03:18	0:02:57
42,195 km	2:03:59	0:00:41

The jobs were in the areas of new housing, SUVs for the rough terrain and even a hotel was under construction. He answered the most important question firmly and laughed: "Yes, everything is ok. I'm coming to Berlin for the fourth time." And we unwrapped the fourth mascot, with which he was a delighted as a child – a Berlin bear, this time a plush. Would it be put in his home museum like the others? He was not sure, as maybe his four year-old son Naty would take a shine to it.

Before we said goodbye, I remembered to pass on a request: Are you coming to Leipzig? It was planned, or rather, hoped, that after the 2008 Berlin Marathon, Haile would visit Leipzig for a day or even two. Although the requestor had written down the reason, it was not so clear to the world record holder: "Why to Leipzig exactly?" So I tried to bring as many possible reasons from Leipzig to Addis Ababa, namely: a few years ago, the cities of Leipzig and Addis Ababa were twinned. This soon led to a lot of activity, including numerous German-Ethiopian encounters, lectures, correspondence, book readings. Sophie Ebert, a member of this busy group, herself an enthusiastic endurance runner, would not give up on her idea of bringing the Ethiopian wonder runner to her home city. So she went to the Ethiopian Embassy in Berlin, used contacts with Leipzigers who were staying in Addis, and also asked me to use my connection with Haile for this project.

I now entered the lobby of the record-holder's massage area. It appeared once again, as I had noticed many times before, that Haile's closest colleagues protected their boss from everything, which is only understandable. I have already mentioned what happens to telephone calls; emails and letters were obviously also 'filtered' though. To get Haile to do something you have to meet him directly, face to face, and then he does not usually like to say no. "A danger for him and his limited time", say his people, and they act accordingly.

He will think about Leipzig, Haile eventually decided. So I let Sophie know that we shall just have to wait and see. For the moment, Haile's fourth Berlin appearance was now imminent.

Followed by cameras after the finish

36th real,-Berlin Marathon, September 20th 2009, 57 – 77°F (14°C – 25°C)

Race director Mark Milde has fielded his best ever line-up for this race. It includes the Kenyan Duncan Kibet, the second fastest marathon runner of all time and also his compatriot Francis Kiprop. But things work out quite differently, and it is ultimately the increasing heat that determines the result. Kibet is unable to repeat his Rotterdam performance of 2:04:27. Disappointment also for Haile, who would have liked to have a strong rival at his side, but he drops out after 32 kilometers due to hip problems. The pacemakers have already dropped out two kilometers earlier. At this point, the Ethiopian was brilliantly positioned, the 1:27:49 constituted a new 30km world record. Afterwards though, the world record holder runs all on his own and wonders many times whether he can stay on track for a new best time. The negative answer is provided by the temperature, now rising to over 68°F (20°C); too hot for new records. Haile's face soon reveals how hard he is struggling and

Haile visits and supports many charity projects at which is usually very hands on. Here he is running with blind children (with a blindfold over his own eyes) in a Christian school in Addis Ababa that was founded with German aid.

Congratulations from the reigning mayor of Berlin, Klaus Wowereit.

how focused he is on winning. Behind him, Kiprop is closing but he has no chance. Haile crosses the finish line in 2:06:08 and, completely exhausted, first leans on a barrier. Just briefly though; then he waves, laughing again and enjoys the victory ceremony. He has won the Berlin Marathon for the fourth time, also breaking the world record on two occasions, an unrivaled achievement that cannot be too highly praised.

In the evening, his supporters could see the four-time champion in a new, unexpected role. Haile not only let it all hang out on the dance floor but also sat at a piano and played an Amharic love song. Then you could have heard a pin drop among the otherwise exuberantly partying marathon men and women.

36th real,-Berlin Marathon, 9.20.2009:
1st Haile Gebrselassie (Eth) 2:06:08,
2nd Francis Kirop (Ken) 2:07:04 3rd Negari Terfa (Eth) 2:07:41

Women:
1st: Atsede Besuye,
2nd Silvia Skvortsova,
3rd Mamitu Daska (Eth) 2:26:38.

Leipzig's the place for me!

The program for the next day was approved. He still hesitated for a long time over whether he was the right person to represent his Ethiopian home city in the German trade fair and sports metropolis. Eventually he said yes; his manager did not disagree. The current and former Berlin Marathon winner, still slightly the worse for wear following the previous day's activities, got into the embassy car after Monday's press conference and drove off to Leipzig with us behind him. The first landmark was the impressive Zentralstacion (central stadium), now restored, then a trip to the Institute for Applied Training Science, and he also gave tips every now and then. For example, for the man on the treadmill: "Bring your arm more across your body." But he also listened attentively too. He was amazed to learn that just one year after the first Olympic Games of 1896, this city had organized a 40km race, making it the starting point of German marathon history. He met a veteran of the modern Leipzig Marathon in Heinrich Hagenloch.

The second destination was the Rathaus (City Hall), in front of which the first Leipzigers had already started to assemble; the news of Haile's visit had been known for days. The media wrote and talked about "Leipzig in Haile Fever." It was a major event for the trade fair and sports city. Leipzig's mayor therefore honored this high-profile visit with an action that not even Berlin itself after four victories of the fastest marathon runner in the world celebrated: he presented the Ethiopian guest with the "Gold Book of Honor" and asked him to sign it. There was applause also from those five runners who had been invited due to their long-standing service.

Then, in front of the steps of the old Rathaus, the mayor gave the starting signal for a symbolic race through the city. Hundreds of runners jogged off; Haile among them. Nobody was bothered by the heat today. The star of Berlin kept to the pace of the average jogger. The finish was the Leipziger Laufladen (Leipzig Running Store), in the Brühl Passage, where the first lines were already forming. Haile stood behind a counter and was prepared to sign autographs of any kind. The protocol had allowed one hour for this, but Haile stayed for two. The enormous crowd could only be controlled because law enforcement officers regulated the influx into the store. He was asked to sign photos, newspapers, books, shoes and running vests. Haile never lost his cool for a moment. He chatted with Jörg, one of the two store owners, while he was writing, and both found they had something in common: when the man from Leipzig won his first marathon around the Auensee lake in 1988, the Ethiopian had merely made the first hundred in his first marathon experiment.

HAILE GEBRSELASSIE

When Haile Gebrselassie won the 2008 Berlin Marathon in world record time, Jörg Mathé had stood on the top of the victory podium of the Leipzig Marathon just a few months earlier.

After an estimated 650 autographs for 450 fans, the running store's glass doors were closed. A press conference followed, which Haile concluded with a piano solo. Would he like to see the famous Monument to the Battle of the Nations now? To this he just kept on smiling and tiredly shook his head. All he wanted now, he replied politely, was to go to his hotel and have a beer. But he would return to Leipzig, perhaps even to compete in the marathon. Sophie, like Haile in the brown attire of the twin town association, promised as a goodbye to race in his Great Ethiopian Run in November with a group, at which he quickly hugged her. "I have to praise this beautiful town", he said. To quote Goethe: "Dieses Leipzig lob ich mir" (Leipzig's the place for me).

Haile Gebrselassie and Jörg Mathé, two marathon champions.

The richest race

Super prizes probably belong to the "Kingdom of Superlatives". Three times, Haile had tried to win the million dollar jackpot of Dubai. The Emirates on the Persian Gulf offered a cool million dollars for a new marathon world record every year. With this sum and a victory prize of $250,000, the wonderland's flat course moved to the top of the marathon prize money list between London and New York.

Three times, the Ethiopian had no problem breaking the tape at the finish, but three times he stopped the clock outside his own world record time. The first time, there was a problem with his pacemakers; they did not run according to plan. The second time the weather put paid to any ambitions. The record was literally rained off. 54°F (12°C) and pouring rain! The temperatures in this city in January are normally between 59 and 72°F (15°C and 22°C), and if it does rain in the desert region, there are just a few drops. Haile still crossed the half marathon point 19 seconds quicker than in the world record hunt of 2008 in Berlin, and even at 30km, he was still looking really good. But then the heavens opened. "I suddenly became a protective shield for everyone behind me", he recalls, and could eventually be more than happy with a time of 2:05:29 in this Dubai downpour. The appearance and prize money were also a good consolation.

One of my favorite signed photos of Haile.

The third Dubai victory also left the world's fastest long distance runner without the hoped-for million dollar record. Several factors were to blame. The high humidity with temperatures at the start of around 68°F (20°C) (the event took place a week earlier than usual), but above all a compacted spine, which the top runner had suffered overnight. A German physiotherapist from

Dubai Marathon, 1.16.2009:
1st Haile Gebrselassie (Eth) 2:05:29 h
2nd Deremsa Chimsa (Eth) 2:07:54 h
3rd Eshetu Wondimu (Eth) 2:08:41 h
Women
1st Bezunesh Bekele (Eth) 2:24:02 h
2nd Atsebe Habtamu (Eth) 2:25:17 h
3rd Helena Kirop (Ken) 2:25:35 h

At the Dubai Marathon, the course runs past the Burj Al Arab, at 1053 feet, the second-highest building in the world.

Detmold, who Haile knew well, was successful. The race started in complete darkness, with Haile present. But then, between the 10 and 15 km marks, a finish without the million dollars looked on the cards. But still his finishing time proved to be the stuff of legend: 2:06:09!

Dubai is always worth visiting for a long-haul running trip, as evidenced by the now more than 10,000 participants in this perfectly organized race, offering 42,195km and 10km. Also thanks to a certain Haile Gebrselassie, the number of entries to the World's Richest Marathon rises year after year. It is quite something to run past the Burj Dubai Tower, at 2,684 feet or the Burj Al Arab, the superhotel at 1,053 feet.

The new "Haile Half Marathon"

In November, nineteen runners from Leipzig were looking forward to the 10th Great Ethiopian Run in Addis Ababa, which had a record 33,000 entries, unequalled in the whole of Africa. The fact that all the guests from Haile's twin town also received invitations to his garden party only increased their sense of anticipation. Haile was not just a star but a man of the people.

And this man kept everyone busy. His Great Ethiopian Run organizers now have several different races to cope with: Ladies' Run, Children's Run, and since May 2010 another new race. He had long ago stopped asking the local Athletics Federation, which was supposed to approve such events. For a long while, he had set up his own Ethiopian running schedule.

Dubai-Marathon, 21.1.2010:
1st Haile Gebrselassie (Eth) 2:06:09 h
2nd Chala Bayene (Eth) 2:06:33 h
3rd Eshetu Wondimu (Eth) 2:06:46 h
Women:
1st Mamitu Daska (Eth) 2:24:18 h
2nd Aberu Shewaye (Eth) 2:24:26 h
3rd Helena Kirop (Ken) 2:24:54 h

He had invited me to this "new development". In Hawassa, about 250 miles south of the capital, beside the wide lake of the same name, he wanted to inaugurate his five star hotel, and as it belonged to him, he thought it should also have running facilities. Its target market was the children and casual runners of the region, as well as international guests. No appearance money, but certificates and small prizes.

It was called "Everyone Race", which although it had been borrowed from a sponsor, was still closely associated with the spirit of running for fun.

It seemed almost impossible to lead Haile away from the debut hoopla for a couple of minutes. Guests had traveled from near and far. Friends and companions. For example, Paul Tergat, the former world record holder from Kenya and Mary Wittenberg, the race director of the New York City Marathon. But that is what he is like, the man without airs and graces, he gave his organizational staff the slip and went off with us. Handwritten dedications on running vests from the earlier Rennsteig Race in Thüringen, Central Germany, the biggest cross country race in Europe. Information about his new hotel, that with more than 112 rooms, two swimming pools, a fitness center and glass-windowed restaurants was one of Ethiopia's most exclusive resorts, and also provided work for 250 people from Hawassa. Finally the inevitable question: would he be racing for the fifth time along the Spree River in Berlin? As he laughingly nodded, we handed him a fifth Berlin bear, at which point his staff urgently reminded him of his duties. A wooden stage had been erected in front of the hotel for the inauguration, from where he addressed around a thousand

Start of the "Haile Half Marathon" in Hawassa, Ethiopia.

Finish of the children's race

Ethiopians from this lake region, constantly interrupted by applause and murmurs of agreement. When Haile talks, he fascinates listeners with his charisma and always gives a clear message. For example: We must all do something to improve our situation, all of us. Everyone, absolutely everyone, according to their possibilities.

Here in front of the gates of his hotel, the following morning he started all the races for children, women, elite pros and casual runners. Almost 3,500 had entered, a respectable result. The highlight was the 21.1km race that we had dubbed the "Haile Half Marathon". With the youngsters, Haile tried a lengthy warm-up. They were also visibly excited about the pink t-shirts for all and the finishers' certificates with the last Berlin victory photo of their role model, who then stood behind the finishing line to welcome them with a handshake.

The most successful of the VIP overseas visitors proved to be Mary Wittenberg, who took third place. Haile was quick to embrace her in the victory ceremony. I assume that later in the post-race party she persuaded him to give Berlin a miss that year and to finally run in the most famous marathon in the world.

"Sorry," he said to me later, pulling a sad face. "We'll see each other at the Brandenberg Gate another time." So we did not ask him to give the fifth bear back…

With Mary Wittenberg, race director of the New York City Marathon on the podium in Hawassa.

The Everyone Race (a.k.a. The Haile Half Marathon) has been held since 2010 on the first Saturday in May in Hawassa, in front of Haile's Resort on Lake Hawassa, about 250 miles south of Addis Ababa and comprises a half marathon, 8km race and a children's race.

View of the new hotel in the extensive "Haile Resort".

The legend lives on

Everything was still going well for him long before New York. All was well in Haile's world. His race schedule included those goals of which he spoke often: Tokyo for example, with whose marathon organizers he had signed a contract, but also Berlin, where the course again inspired him to try for a new record. And of course, London 2012 – Abebe Bikila and Mamo Wolde send their regards. An Olympic marathon victory would mean another crown for the running emperor. Certainly the most brilliant of all the many, almost innumerable trophies.

Yes, he still had plenty of dreams. The man who once stepped out of a simple Ethiopian village into the complicated world, where he soon found success that earned him the title 'the greatest runner of all time', which he had not sought but was forced to accept, could also be serious and reflective. At these times, his smile briefly disappeared. For example when he said: "I know that many people are still watching me. That is not an easy burden, it is a responsibility. I will be measured in everything that I do; many people are watching me. I must always be on the right path, can never lose and can never make a mistake. But I am just a man, who doesn't always get everything right. But I say again: believe me that everything I do, I do for my country, for Ethiopia."

In the days before the New York Marathon, the world looked rather different though. More knee pain, already on the outward flight. Not starting was out of the question, he was looking forward to the celebrated race and to meeting Mary Wittenberg, the race director, whose invitation to race he had accepted in Hawassa. But the thoughts could not be banished as easily as bothersome flies. How often had injuries appeared when a decisive victory was at stake? It was a recurring theme in Haile's racing history: In each Olympic race he had had to struggle against injuries, in the London Marathon his old asthma problems returned, in the last Dubai Marathon it was the turn of his back. Even in October, he had to cancel his planned trip to Berlin due to breathing problems, where he wanted to open an exhibition of 3,500 boxes of Listros, the Ethiopian shoe polishers on the *Potsdamer Platz* together with the President of Germany. These original Ethiopian shoe-polishing boxes represented the dreams, ideas and messages of each child and young person who had a daily struggle for survival. For 5 Birr, about 50 cents, a day.

Haile's New York Marathon debut on November 7th, 2010 ended after only 25km, at which point he was finally forced to recognize that his body could take no more. His right knee was so painful that he left the leading group and stood at the side of the road. Later, the cause was diagnosed to be fluid in the knee.

Out, but only of this race that he actually wanted to win? He was frustrated. When the 37-year-old world record-holder appeared before reporters, he could not hide a couple of tears in his eyes. "I am disappointed in myself", he said, with no trace of his famous smile. "It's better to stop here." He stood up from the wooden chair and wanted to go. One reporter ventured: "Does that mean that you want to retire?" To which he just replied: "Yes."

It took the reporters a while to understand what was happening, and they prepared lengthy articles that read like obituaries: "The King abdicates," "Goodbye to the best distance runner of all time," "The End of an Era." The President of the International Association of Athletics Federations had only prepared three words in all the excitement: "Sporting hero, genius, legend." Mark Milde, the Berlin Marathon race director, did not want to believe it and classified the "retirement" as a "kneejerk reaction." The Dutch manager Jos Hermens, whom Haile had not told of his decision, was still on the course when he heard the news and thought it was a joke. There was a lot he was no longer able to discuss with his friend and protegé, whose international career he had guided for years. Haile got on the next plane and jetted off home to Addis Ababa. To his family where he sought and found consolation.

My own attempts to reach him by phone were unsuccessful, as expected. Haile had completely cut himself off. My friend Amanuel, who was very close to him, also tried in vain in Addis Ababa and told me: "Ethiopia is in mourning. The people here don't understand it. For them he is an icon; everybody thinks that he must run and live forever." The only one to be able to contact him was Jos Hermens. He spent a long time on the phone with him, comforted him and reminded him of his heavenly dreams and earthly contracts. In any case, he was finally able to express his hope as follows to the AP news agency in Brussels: "I believe that Haile is not hanging up his running shoes for good and will keep going for the London Olympics. He told me he is going to think about it. I think that the shock of his New York withdrawal led him to this precipitated decision."

Whatever happens, one thing is certain; the legend lives on. Even if one great dream bursts like a bubble, the fame of the Ethiopian wonder runner and philanthropist will never fade. On the desk in his office, high above Addis Ababa, stands a framed greeting from a fan. It is not easy to see, as it is slightly hidden by his computer, printer and fax machine. I imagine that Haile looks at it every so often:
"Dear Haile", it says, "You are always our HERO!!!!"

The race of destiny? A new kid on the block? On November 7th, 2010 in New York, the 26 year-old Ethiopian Gebre Gebremariam won his first ever marathon in 2:08:14. His famous compatriot Haile Gebrselassie dropped out.

SWEDEN
FENNASSI
ING 1-001
MODESTO
ING 1-091
HAILE
Reebok
TORRES
USA
RITZ
USA
MEB
MARILSON

Ethiopia, a general overview

7 Milestones (Statistics)

Haile's track record

A selection of his most notable races:

1988 (1 race)

6.19: Abebe Bikila Marathon, Addis Ababa, 2:48 – 99th.

1991 (2 races)

3.24: World Junior Cross Country Championships 8,420m, Antwerp, Belgium, 24:23 – 8th .

1992 (4 races)

3.21: World Junior Cross-Country Championships 8,000m, Boston, USA 23:36 – 2nd .

9.18: World Junior Championships 10K, Seoul, South Korea, 28:03.99 – 1st place.

9.19: World Junior Championships 5K, Seoul, South Korea, 13:36.06 – 1st.

11.8: Ekiden Relays 5K, Berlin, Germany 13:24 – 1st.

1993 (18 races)

8.16: World Championships 5K, Stuttgart, Germany 13:03.17 – 2nd.

8.22: World Championships 10K, Stuttgart, Germany 27:26.02 – 1st.

1994 (15 races)

3.26: World Cross Country Championships 12,060m, Budapest, Hungary 34:32 – 3rd.

6.4: Adriaan Paulen Memorial 5K, Hengelo, Holland 12:56.96 – 1st.

7.6: Athletissima 10K, Lausanne, Switzerland 27:15.00 –1st.

1995 (12 races)

5.27: Kerkrade Classics 2 Miles, Kerkrade, Holland 8:07.46 – 1st.

6.5: Adriaan Paulen Memorial 10K, Hengelo, Holland 26:43.53 – 1st.

8.8: World Championships 10K, Gothenberg, Sweden 27:12.95 – 1st.

8.16: Zürich Grand Prix 5K, Switzerland 12:44.39 – 1st.

9.1: ISTAF Grand Prix 5K, Berlin, Germany 12:53.19 – 1st.

HAILE GEBRSELASSIE

1996 (10 races)

5.19: Leichtathletik Meeting 1,500m, Chemnitz, Germany 3:34.64 – 1st.

7.29: Olympic Games 10K, Atlanta, USA 27:07.34 – 1st.

1997 (17 races)

2.9: Leichtathletik Meeting 800m, Dortmund, Germany 1:49.35 – 1st.

2.20: Indoor Meeting 5K, Stockholm, Sweden 12:59.04 – 1st.

3.9: World Indoor Championships 3,000m, Paris, France 7:34.71 – 1st.

5.31: Adriaan Paulen Memorial 2 miles, Hengelo, Holland 8:01.08 – 1st.

7.4: Bislett Games 10K, Oslo, Norway 26:31.32 – 1st.

8.6: World Championships 10K, Athens, Greece 27:24.58 – 1st.

8.13: Zürich Grand Prix 5K, Switzerland 12:41.86 – 1st.

8.22: Leichtathletik-Meeting 2,000m, Brussels, Belgium 4:56.10 – 1st.

8.26: ISTAF Grand Prix 5K, Berlin, Germany 12:55.14 – 1st.

1998 (18 races)

1.25: Indoor Meeting 3,000m, Karlsruhe, Germany 7:26.14 – 1st.

2.15: Indoor Meeting 2,000m, Birmingham, GB 4:52.86 – 1st.

6.1: Adriaan Paulen Memorial 10K, Hengelo, Holland 26:22.75 – 1st.

6.13: Grand Prix 5K, Helsinki, Finland 12:39.36 – 1st.

8.28: Van Damme Memorial 3,000m, Brussels, 7:25.09 – 1st.

9.1: ISTAF Grand Prix 5K, Berlin, Germany 12:56.52 – 1st.

Joint winner of the Golden League

1999 (16 races)

2.14: Indoor Grand Prix 5K, Birmingham, GB 12:50.38 – 1st.

3.5: World Indoor Championships 3,000m, Maebashi, Japan 7:53.57 – 1st.

3.7: World Indoor Championships 1,500m, Maebashi, Japan 3:33.77 – 1st.

6.6: Leichtathletik-Meeting 1,500m, Stuttgart, Germany 3:33.73 – 1st.

6.27: British Grand Prix 1 mile, Gateshead, GB 3:52.39 – 1st.

8.24: World Championships 10K, Seville, Spain 27:57.27 – 1st.

2000 (6 races)

9.25: Olympic Games 10K, Sydney, Australia 27:18.20 – 1st.

2001 (7 races)

8.8: World Championships 10K, Edmonton, Canada 27:54.41 – 3rd.

8.26: Ethiopian Half Marathon Championships, Addis Ababa, 1:04:34 – 1st.

10.7: World Half Marathon Championships, Bristol, GB 1:00:03 – 1st.

2002 (5 races)

3.24: Lisbon Half Marathon, Portugal, 59:40 – 1st.

4.14: London Marathon, GB 2:06:35 – 3rd.

6.1: One Hour Run, Hengelo, Holland, dropped out.

12.11: 10km road race, Doha, Qatar 27:02 – 1st.

2003 (10 races)

2.21: Indoor Grand Prix 2 miles, Birmingham, GB 8:04.69 – 1st.

3.16: World Indoor Championships 3,000m, Birmingham, GB 7:40.97 – 1st.

8.24: World Championships 10K, Paris, France, 26:50.77 – 2nd.

9.5: Van Damme Memorial 10K, Brussels, Belgium, 26:29.22 – 1st.

2004 (6 races)

8.20: Olympic Games 10K, Athens, Greece, 27:27.70 – 5th.

2005 (2 races)

9.4: Tilburg Ten Miles, Holland 44:24 – 1st.

10.16: Amsterdam Marathon, 2:06:20 – 1st. (30km split 1:58:57)

2006 (5 races)

1.15: Rock´n-Roll Half Marathon, Phoenix/Tempe, USA, 58:55 – 1st. (20km split 55:48)

3.12: 25km, Alphen aan den Rijn, Holland, 1:11:32 – 1st.

4.16: London Marathon, GB, 2:09:05 – 9th.

9.24: Berlin Marathon, Germany, 2:05:56 – 1st.

12.13: Fukuoka Marathon, Japan, 2:06:52 – 1st.

2007 (5 races)

4.22: London Marathon, GB – did not participate

5.26:10K Hengelo, Holland 26:52.33 – 5th.

6.27: Golden Spikes, Ostrava, Czech Republic, 20km 56:25:98, One Hour run 21,285m World Record

8.5: Half Marathon New York, USA 59:24 – 1st.

9.30: Berlin Marathon, Germany 2:04:26 – 1st.

2008 (5 races)

1.18: Dubai Marathon, UAE, 2:04:53 – 1st.

3.16: Lisbon Half Marathon, Portugal, 59:15 – 1st.

5.24: 10K Hengelo, Holland 26:51.20 – 2nd.

8.17: Olympic Games 10K, Beijing, China, 27:06.68 – 6th.

9.28: Berlin Marathon, 2:03:59 - 1st.

2009 (6)

16.1.: Dubai-Marathon, 2:05:29 - 1st.

14.3.: Den Haag, Half Marathon: 59:50 - 2nd.

17.5.: Manchester, 10km road race, 27:39 - 1st.

1.6.: Hengelo, Half Marathon 59:49 - 2nd.

20.9.: Berlin Marathon, Germany, 2:06:08 – 1st.

12.31: 8km New Year's Eve City Run, Trier, Germany, 22:23 – 1st.

2010

1.23: Dubai Marathon, UAE 2:06:09 – 1st.

3.21: New York Half Marathon – did not participate

5.16: Manchester, GB 10km road race, 28:02 – 1st.

9.19: Great North Run, Newcastle, Half Marathon: 59:33 min – 1st.

11.7: New York Marathon – dropped out

Haile's world best times

1.) 5K **12:56.96** (6.4.94 Hengelo, Netherlands)

2.) 2 Miles 8:07.46 (5.27.95 Kerkrade, Netherlands)

3.) 10K **26:43.53** (6.5.95 Hengelo, Netherlands)

4.) 5K **12:44.39** (8.16.95 Zurich, Switzerland)

5.) 5K Indoors **13:10.98** (1.27.96 Sindelfingen, Germany)

6.) 3,000m Indoors **7:30.72** (2.4.96 Stuttgart, Germany)

7.) 5K Indoors **12:59.04** (2.20.97 Stockholm, Sweden)

8.) 2 Miles 8:01.08 (5.31.97 Hengelo, Netherlands)

9.) 10K **26:31.32** (7.4.97 Oslo, Norway)

10.) 5K **12:41.86** (8.13.97 Zurich, Switzerland)

11.) 3,000m Indoors **7:26.14** (1.25.98 Karlsruhe, Germany)

12.) 10K **26:22.75** (6.1.98 Hengelo, Netherlands)

13.) 2,000m 4:52.86 (2.15.98 Birmingham, GB)

14.) 5K **12:39.36** (6.13.98 Helsinki, Finland)

15.) 5K Indoors **12:50.38** (2.14.99 Birmingham, GB)

16.) 10km road race **27:02** (12.11.02 Doha, Qatar)

18.) 2 Miles 8:04.69 (2.21.03 Birmingham, GB)

19.) 15km 41:22 (9.4.05 Tilburg, Netherlands)

20.) 10 Miles 44:24 (9.4.05 Tilburg, Netherlands)

21.) 30km 1:28:57 (10.16.05 during Amsterdam Marathon, Netherlands)

22.) 20km **55:48** (1.15.06 Phoenix/Tempe, USA, during Half Marathon)

23.) Half Marathon **58:55** (1.15.06 Phoenix/Tempe, USA)

24.) 25km 1:11:37 (3.12.06 Alphen aan den Rijn, Netherlands)

25.) 20km track **56:25:98** (6.27.07 Ostrava, Czech Republic)

26.) 1 Hour run **21,285**m (6.27.07 Ostrava, Czech Republic)

27.) Marathon **2:04:26** (9.30.07 Berlin, Germany)

28.) 30km 1:27:49 (9.28.2008 Berlin, Germany, during Marathon)

29.) Marathon **2:03:59** (9.28.2008, Berlin, Germany)
(in bold – ratified as World Records)

Haile's Marathons

1.) Abebe Bikila Marathon 2:48, Addis Ababa 6.19.88 – 99th.

2.) London Marathon 2:06:35. 4.14.02 – 3rd.

3.) Amsterdam Marathon, Netherlands 2:06:20, 10.16.05 – 1st.

4.) London Marathon, GB 2:09:05, 4.16.06 – 9th.

5.) Berlin Marathon, Germany, 2:05:56, 9.24.06 – 1st.

6.) Fukuoka Marathon, Japan, 2:06:52, 12.3.06 – 1st.

7.) London Marathon, GB, 4.22.07 – did not participate

8.) Berlin Marathon, Germany 2:04:26, 9.30.07 – 1st. (WR)

9.) Dubai Marathon, UAE, 2:04:53, 1.18.08 – 1st.

10.) Berlin Marathon, Germany, 2:03:59, 9.28.08 – 1st. (WR)

11.) Dubai Marathon, UAE, 2:05:29, 1.16.09 – 1st.

12.) Berlin Marathon, Germany, 2:06:08, 9.20.09 – 1st.

13.) Dubai Marathon, UAE, 2:06:09, 1.23.10 – 1st.

14.) New York Marathon 11.7.10 – dropped out

Some Marathon facts

The Pioneers

Men

1886 First under 3:00 (40km): Spiridon Louis (Gre) 2:58:50

1913 First under 2:40 h: Harry Green (GB) 2:38:17

1925 First under 2:30 h: Albert Michelsen (USA) 2:29:02

1953 First under 2:20 h: Jim Peters (GB) 2:18:41

1967 First under 2:10 h: Derek Clayton (Aus) 2:09:37

1969 First under 2:09 h: Derek Clayton (Aus) 2:08:34

1985 First under 2:08 h: Carlos Lopes (Por) 2:07:12

1988 First under 2:07 h: Belayneh Dinsamo (Eth) 2:06:50

1999 First under 2:06 h: Khalid Khannouchi (Mar) 2:05:42

2003 First under 2:05 h: Paul Tergat (Ken) 2:04:55

2008 First under 2:04 h: Haile Gebrselassie (Eth) 2:03:59

Women

1971 First under 3:00 h: Beth Bonner (USA) 2:55:22

1979 First under 2:30 h: Grete Waitz (Nor) 2:27:33

1983 First under 2:25 h: Joan Benoit (USA) 2:22:43

2001 First under 2:20 h: Naoko Takahashi (Jap) 2:19:46

2002 First under 2:18 h: Paula Radcliffe (GB) 2:17:18

2003 First under 2:16 h: Paula Radcliffe (GB) 2:15:25

Marathon record progression

World Best Times/World Records

Men

2:55:18 John Hayes (USA) London 7.24.1908

2:52:45 Roy Fowler (USA) New York 1909

2:46:52 James Clark (USA) New York 2.12.1909

2:46:04 Albert Raine (USA) New York 12.12.1909

2:42:31 Fred Barrett (GB) London 12.15.1909

2:38:16 Harry Green (GB) London 5.12.1913

2:36:06 Alexis Ahlgren (Sweden) London 5.13.1913

2:32:35 Hannes Kolehmainen (Fin) Antwerp, Belgium 8.22.1920

2:29:01 Albert Michelsen (USA) Port Chester 10.12.1925

2:27:49 Fusashige Suzuki (Jap) Tokyo 5.31.1935

2:26:44 Yasuo Ikenaka (Jap) Tokyo 4.3.1935

2:25:39 Yun Bok Suh (Kor) Boston 4.19.1947

2:20:42 James Peters (GB) Cheswick 6.14.1952

2:18:40 James Peters (GB) Cheswick 6.13.1953

2:18:34 James Peters (GB) Turku 10.4.1953

2:17:39 James Peters (GB) Cheswick 6.26.1954

2:15:17 Sergej Popow (SU) Stockholm 8.24.1958

2:15:16 Abebe Bikila (Eth) Rom 9.10.1960

2:15:15 Toru Terasawa (Jap) Beppu 2.17.1963

2:14:28 Leonard Edelen (USA) Cheswick 6.15.1963

2:13:55 Basil Heatley (GB) Cheswick 6.13.1964

2:12:11 Abebe Bikila (Eth) Tokyo 10.21.1964

2:12:00 Mono Shigematsu (Jap) 6.12.1965

2:09:36 Derek Clayton (Aus) Fukuoka 12.3.1967

2:08:34 Derek Clayton (Aus) Antwerp 5.30.1969

2:08:18 Robert de Castella (Aus) Fukuoka 12.6.1981

2:08:05 Steve Jones (USA) Chicago 10.21.1984

2:07:12 Carlos Lopes (Por) Rotterdam 4.17.1988

2:06:05 Belaine Dinsamo (Eth) Rotterdam 4.17.1988

2:06:05 Ronaldo da Costa (Bra) Berlin 9.20.1998

2:05:42 Khalid Khannouchi (Mar) Chicago 10.24.10.1999

2:05:38 Khalid Khannouchi (Mar) London 14.4.2002

2:04:55 Paul Tergat (Ken) Berlin 9.24.2004

2:04:26 Haile Gebrselassie (Eth) Berlin 9.30.2007

2:03:59 Haile Gebrselassie (Eth) Berlin 9.28.2008

Women

3:40:22 Violet Piercy (GB) Windsor/London 10.3.1926

3:37:07 Merry Lepper (USA) Culver City 12.16.1963

3:27:45 Dale Greg (GB) Ryde 5.23.1964

3:19:33 Mildred Sampson (Aus) Auckland 7.21.1964

3:15:22 Maureen Wilton (Kan) Toronto 5.6.1967

3:0726 Anni Pede-Erdkamp (Ger) Waldniel 9.16.1967

3:02:53 Caroline Walker (USA) Seaside 2.28.1970

3:01:42 Elizabeth Bonner (USA) Philadelphia 5.9.1971

3:00:35 Sara Mae Berman (USA) Brockton 5.30.1971

2:55:22 Elizabeth Bonner (USA) New York 9.19.1971

2:49:40 Cheryl Bridges (USA) Culver City 12.5.1971

2:46:36 Michiko Gorman (USA) Culver City 12.2.1973

2:46:24 Chantal Langlacé (Fra) Neuf Brisach 10.27.1974

2:43:54 Jacqueline Hansen (USA) Culver City 12.1.1974

2:42:42 Liane Winter (D) Boston 4.21.1975

2:40:15 Christa Vahlensieck (Ger) Dülmen 5.3.1975

2:38:19 Jacqueline Hansen (USA) Eugene 10.21.1975

2:35:15 Chantal Langlacé (Fra) Oyarzun 5.1.1977

2:34:47 Christa Vahlensieck (Ger) Berlin 9.10.1977

2:32:29 Grete Waitz (Nor) New York 10.22.1978

2:27:32 Grete Waitz (Nor) New York 10.21.1979

2:25:41 Grete Waitz (Nor) New York 10.26.1980

2:25:28 Grete Waitz (Nor) London 4.17.1983

2:22:42 Joan Benoit (USA) Boston 4.18.1983

2:21:06 Ingrid Kristiansen (Nor) London 10.21.1985

2:20:47 Tegla Loroupe (Ken) Rotterdam 4.19.1998

2:20:43 Tegla Loroupe (Ken) Berlin 9.26.1999

2:19:46 Naoko Takahashi (Jap) Berlin 9.30.2001

2:18:47 Catherine Ndereba (Ken) Chicago 10.7.2001

2:17:18 Paula Radcliffe (GB) Chicago 10.13.2002

2:15:25 Paula Radcliffe (GB) London 4.13.2003

The most successful Marathon runners of all time

Double Olympic Champions:

Abebe Bikila (Eth) 1960 and 1964

Waldemar Cierpinski (GDR) 1976 and 1980

Double World Champions:

Abel Anton (Spa) 1997 and 1999

Jaouad Gharib (Mor) 2003 and 2005

Olympic Marathon champions

Men

1896 Spiridon Louis (Gre)

1900 Michel Theato (Fra)

1904 Thomas Hicks (USA)

1908 John Hayes (USA)

1912 Kenneth Mc Arthur (SAf)

1920 Hannes Kohlemainen (Fin)

1924 Albin Stenroos (Fin)

1928 Boughera El Ouafi (Fra)

1932 Juan Carlos Zabala (Arg)

1936 Sohn Kee-Chung (Jap)

1948 Delfo Cabrera (Arg)

1952 Emil Zatopek (Cze)

1956 Alain Momoun (Fra)

1960 Abebe Bikila (Eth)

1964 Abebe Bikila (Eth)

1968 Mamo Wolde (Eth)

1972 Frank Shorter (USA)

1976 Waldemar Cierpinski (GDR)

1980 Waldemar Cierpinski (GDR)

1984 Carlos Lopes (Por)

1988 Gelindo Bordin (Ita)

1992 Hwang Young-Cho (Kor)

1996 Josia Thugwane (SAf)

2000 Abera Gezahegne (Eth)

2004 Stefano Baldini (Ita)

2008 Samuel Wanjiru (Ken)

Women

1984 Joan Benoit (USA)

1988 Rosa Mota (Por)

1992 Valentina Yegorowa (Unified Team)

1996 Fatuma Roba (Eth)

2000 Naoko Takahashi (Jap)

2004 Mizuki Noguchi (Jap)

2008 Constantina Tomescu (Rom)

The most successful Olympic Marathon nations

Ethiopia 5 Gold/3 Bronze

USA 4 Gold/2 Silver/6 Bronze

Japan 3 Gold/3 Silver/3 Bronze

France 3 Gold/1 Silver

South Africa 2 Gold/2 Silver

Italy 2 Gold/1 Silver/1 Bronze

Argentina 2 Gold/1 Silver

Finland 2 Gold/3 Bronze

Germany 2 Gold/2 Bronze

Portugal 2 Gold/1 Bronze

Kenya 1 Gold/4 Silver/2 Bronze

N.B.: 1x Gold, 1x Bronze were won in 1936 by 2 Koreans for Japan; Korea had been annexed. 2 German Gold medals und 1 Bronze medal were won by GDR athletes.

Ethiopian Olympic Medals

1956 (Melbourne):	Debut with 12 Athletes. No medals.
1960 (Rome):	Gold Marathon Abebe Bikila
	(First African Olympic Champion)
1964 (Tokyo):	Gold Marathon Abebe Bikila
1968 (Mexico City):	Gold Marathon Mamo Wolde
	Silver 10K Mamo Wolde
1972 (Munich):	Bronze 10K Miruts Yifter
	Bronze Marathon Mamo Wolde
1976 (Montreal):	Ethiopia did not take part
1980 (Moscow):	Gold 5K Miruts Yifter
	Gold 10K Miruts Yifter
1984 (Los Angeles):	Ethiopia did not take part
1988 (Soul):	Ethiopia did not take part
1992 (Barcelona):	Gold 10K (W) Derartu Tulu
	Bronze 5K Fita Bayisa
	Bronze 10K Addis Ababa
1996 (Atlanta):	Gold 10K Haile Gebrselassie
	Gold Marathon (W) Fatuma Roba
	(First female African Olympic Marathon Champion)
	Bronze 10K (W) Gete Wami
2000 (Sydney):	Gold 5K Million Wolde
	Gold 10K Haile Gebrselassie
	Gold Marathon Gezahgne Abera
	Gold 10K (W) Derartu Tulu
	Silver 10K (W) Gete Wami
	Bronze 5K (W) Gete Wami
	Bronze Marathon Tesfaye Tola

2004 (Athens):	Gold 10K Kenenisa Bekele
	Gold 5K (W) Meseret Defar
	Silver 5K Kenenisa Bekele
	Silver 10K Sileshi Sihine
	Silver 10K (W) Ejegayehu Dibaba
	Bronze 10K (W) Derartu Tulu
2008 (Beijng):	Gold 10K (W) Tirunesh Dibaba
	Gold 5K (W) Tirunesh Dibaba
	Gold 10K Kenenisa Bekele
	Gold 5K Kenenisa Bekele
	Silver 10K Sileshi Sihine
	Bronze 5000m (W) Meseret Defar
	Bronze Marathon Tsegaye Kebede

8 Last Leg

(written after Haile's world record in 2007)

Haile – in a class of his own

By Dr. David Martin

Those of us back in the pack find such a finish time for a marathon footrace rather unfathomable. Run around that 400m track once in 70.8 seconds, and now do this 104 more times without taking a break, and you'll still be tied with Geb – but you'll have to continue onward at that pace for another half lap to the finish.

Another interesting question is "which of Gebrselassie's records is the best?" In order to compare each of the races, one must find a way to analyze 16 different combinations of running surface (road and track), environment (indoors and out), and distance (from 3,000 m to marathon). The science of exercise physiology provides a tool for comparative assessment of the outdoor competitions.

Dr. David Martin, emeritus Professor of the University of Atlanta, USA, is AIMS statistician and coach of the US distance runners. His article on Haile's world best performances appeared in "Distance Running."

When we exercise, our breathing quickens and deepens. This brings oxygen into the working muscles and allows metabolism to produce energy for muscle movement. The largest volume of oxygen that can be absorbed and utilized is a quantity called VO_2-max. The units of this quantity are volume of oxygen in milliliters per kilogram of body weight, per minute. VO_2-max is partly determined by genetics, partly by running efficiency, but also by training – running distances at a faster pace tends to raise one's VO_2-max.

Notice that Geb's 10K Hengelo performance in June of 1998, as well as his 5,000m race two weeks later at Helsinki, appear to be his best efforts to date. Working at a metabolic rate (represented as VO_2- max in ml/kg/min) of 84.7 ml/kg/min, this brought finish times of 26:22.75 for 10000m and 12:39.36 for 5000m. Note also, however, that Geb's 2:04:26 at Berlin, despite being 29 seconds faster than Tergat's then existing record, required a slightly smaller VO_2-max value

(82.4) than the 84.7 value for the two track performances. What do the performance tables say that Geb could have run for the marathon while working at an energy level of 84.7 ml/kg/min? The answer is an astonishing 2:01:32!

My prediction from analyzing mountains of marathon finish times is that this two-hour barrier will not be broken before 2015. And Geb will likely have retired before then. But his charismatic smile and effortless style of running will do much to bring the best out of his competitors as the next group tries to emulate this "greatest distance runner ever."

Nobody is as memorable

By Mark Milde

The Berlin Marathon has seen many running stars come and go: Uta Pippig, Tegla Loroupe, Naoko Takahashi, Paul Tergat, but none has been as memorable as Haile Gebrselassie. He has a special aura, no airs and graces, and manages to get the crowd on his side like nobody else. He does it in a natural way though, which is unrivalled.

Mark Milde was race director of the Berlin Marathon at the time of Haile's victories between 2006 and 2009. He is the son of Horst Milde, founder and race director until 2003. He was previously responsible for attracting top athletes.

Being able to run fast is one thing, but not everyone can also impress with their personality. He has managed to attract the attention of the world's public and has become one of the few world class African stars. It is inevitable that a runner enchants his own compatriots, but the fact that even Berliners who know nothing about the marathon recognize him on the street and talk to him in the summer, is something you don't see every day. Geb's previous appearances at the Berlin Marathon have therefore always been special occasions that I like to look back on. Even though in his first attempt he didn't break the world record in the marathon (the sport's blue ribbon event), his second run led to his desired entry into the history books. The meticulously planned, excellent pace making between 10 and 30km was the foundation of what was then the fastest marathon of all time. The last 12km saw an impressive solo run from Geb, and he crossed the line in 2:04:26, thus proving that he had now also mastered the marathon. We are proud of the role we have played in helping to make him the greatest runner of all time.

HAILE GEBRSELASSIE

True greatness in defeat

By Manfred Steffny

Even Haile's teacher asked him why he laughed so often. The schoolboy could only shrug his shoulders. It was just how he was, friendly and open, seeing the positive side of everything. Even in his few defeats.

Manfred Steffny, publisher and editor in chief of the running magazine "Spiridon", participated in the Olympic Marathon in Mexico City, 1968 (17th place).

Great sporting champions have often proved to be bad losers, especially at the end of their careers. There have even been cases where stars have forced a dangerous opponent out of their race in a track and field meet in order to avoid being beaten. Not Haile. He has risen to every challenge, even if it was touch and go in a race due to illness or injury. He fearlessly threw himself into the fray and so was still able to respect himself.

The 2001 World Athletics Championships in Edmonton were a case in point. Haile had already been World 10k champion four times in a row. Laughing, he held up five fingers to running colleagues and reporters. He wanted to win a fifth title. Nobody doubted that he could. Only Haile and his closest circle knew that he had a fever and was desperately fighting to be fit. In the race itself, the usual Ethiopian team tactics prevailed, which meant Assefa Mezegebu and Ybeltal Amassu swapping the lead with Haile in their wake. Both were so careful to carry Haile to the hunt like a leopard that they passed up their own chances. In the last lap, the Kenyan Charles Kamathi suddenly stepped up, overtook the three Ethiopians and took the title. Haile only finished third.

What happened in Edmonton should never happen again. Haile too believed that the important thing was to win for his country and not for himself. In the World Championships year 2003, a new star was shooting across the running skies: Kenenisa Bekele, the invincible world cross country champion, but with no experience at all of track racing and its rules, in the hotel for days on end, when talking to journalists, where he sat there shyly, he only spoke Amharic. Haile's true human greatness was now revealed; he looked after him, played the interpreter and explicitly declared him to be his successor. Of course Haile wanted to be world 10K champion again in Paris in 2003, but there were no tactics, no agreement. Ethiopia's head coach Dr. Woldemeskel

Kostre wanted to have two irons in the fire. It proved to be an exciting race that was narrowly won by the younger man. Haile generously raised the arms of his nemesis immediately after the finish. “Look, this is our next great star!” He jubilantly ran a lap of honor next to the reserved Kenenisa Bekele and in the press conference gave the impression of a fair athlete who had lost to a better man.

Perhaps he had reminded Haile of himself in his younger days, for whom victory at international level was really not made easy. In the World Junior Championships in Seoul in 1992, after the clear win over 10K, he became involved in a tussle on the finishing straight with the soon to be 5K world champion Ismail Kirui from Kenya. The Kenyan demanded Haile’s disqualification. There was a lot of anger, but Haile remained double world junior champion. Similarly in 1993, in his first World Championships win in the senior competition in Stuttgart, Haile was said to have trodden on the shoe of leading Kenyan Moses Tanui...Way before anyone else, Haile saw that he could not defeat Bikila on the track and was therefore already planning to move up to the marathon. He made his first attempt in London in 2002. In a great race, Khalid Khannouchi broke the world record in a terrific sprint finish down the Mall, also beating Paul Tergat in the process, Haile’s eternal rival who had become his friend. Haile took third place in London in 2:06:35, an unofficial world’s best time for a marathon debut!

His laugh deserted him then in the Olympic 10K final in Athens. He looked crestfallen as he crossed the line in fifth, while Bekele was already celebrating on the final bend. In the last lap, he had been left standing because of the pain in his foot. Haile tortured himself further with a lap of honor. A little later came the second Achilles tendon operation. But the thirty-something athlete was now working hard on his comeback on the roads. His manager Jos Hermens brokered a highly paid several-year contract with the London Marathon. But in April 2006, despite the best preparation and an adjustment to his running style, he could only finish 9th. “Ninth; that is the worst result of my life”, he berated himself. Anyone else would have thought about hanging up their spikes, but not Haile. In October of the same year, he ran the best time in the world that year in Amsterdam and was again the talk of the running world. In 2006, he famously just missed Paul Tergat’s world record. His runs above Addis Ababa became longer. He felt in great shape. But then the inconceivable happened in London 2007: he dropped out at 30km, before the race had really got going. He couldn’t breathe, he said later, which did not stop him from giving a friendly greeting to Londoners as he said goodbye. The setback was unexplained, until doctors found out that Haile suffered from a pollen allergy to plants that were prevalent in England. Six weeks later, Haile ran in a 10K race in Hengelo without any track training at all. Seat cushions with his likeness on had been distributed around the stands. After all, he had set two world records here. Even though Sileshi Sihine won in front of Eliud Kipchoge, the acclaimed hero was the real winner, Haile finished fifth in 26:52.81 in marathon shoes. This restored his self-confidence.

Haile is never afraid of defeat, and of losing face. He has always had the last laugh. As in the 2008 African Championships in Addis Ababa, when a few minutes before the start of the 5K race, he was awarded an Honorary Doctorate for International Understanding by the University of Leeds and, instead of making a dignified return to the stands, he spontaneously decided on a lap of honor with gown and mortarboard in front of 3,500 spectators.

Always a challenge

By Paul Tergat

Paul Tergat, Kenya, world cross country champion 1995-99, Olympic silver medallist in 1996 and 2000 over 10K, marathon world record in 2003 92:04:55), born on June 17th 1969, member of the army, married with 3 children.

I think it was bad luck, especially in Sydney. When the difference is one second, you have to accept that the other man was better. But a few hundredths – that is different… I accept that Haile had more luck in the Olympics than I, but I am not bitter. I am not the only one who lacks the Olympic crown. Wilson Kipketer dominated the 800m for a decade, but he never won an Olympic gold medal. Moses Kiptanui also, the king of the steeplechase. That is sport.

I respect Haile very much for what he has achieved. He is a great champion, and also a good friend. I have been to his house in Addis Ababa and he came to see me in Nairobi in 2004. I feel a lot of sympathy for him. I also know that he has always trained very, very hard, perhaps even harder than me. Haile was the one who always challenged me to do more, in all the years since I have been an international athlete. He helped me to stay motivated. I believe that without him I would not have achieved what I have. But I am also convinced that he also benefited equally from our rivalry.

Africa's smile

By Wolfgang Weising

Africa has many faces. Almost omnipresent are those that show hunger and misery. And then there are those faces that depict the hope and awakening of the Dark Continent into the world. Alongside the righteous in the mold of Nelson Mandela, or other outstanding African women and men, there are frequently athletes who embody Africa's strength and hope. One of them is undoubtedly Haile Gebrselassie, the wonder runner from Ethiopia.

Wolfgang Weising, Editor in Chief of the magazine Laufzeit (time for running), ambitious distance runner, member of the Berlin Marathon organizing committee.

Sports fans and experts know only too well that in sport there are no miracles. Even altitude and genetic make-up alone cannot account for it. As well as talent, character is also required to develop it. Tenacity and an indefatigable dedication to training also form the foundation of Haile Gebrselassie's running success. The number of world records he has set is unparalleled in the history of sport. But the likeable and always friendly man has long been more than just a sporting success. He is now a successful businessman and an established family man. He is dedicated to helping his Ethiopian homeland, one of the poorest nations on earth, in many ways. For example, he has financed several schools with his running prize money. His firm provides work for people.

His charm and his witty humor, his urbane approach to press conferences on the sidelines of his running appearances all over the world show one of the most charismatic faces of modern Africa.

HAILE GEBRSELASSIE

It is quite simply Africa's smile. His actions give his country a little hope. He is now more popular than anyone else in his homeland. Some would even want to elect him President. He is also an idol for the young people.

If double Olympic marathon champion Abebe Bikila started to write Ethiopian sporting history, Haile Gebrselassie took the baton from him and is now taking it into a totally new dimension.

Such a man deserves our heartfelt wishes for further success and, why not, for eternal life so that he can continue to do good. Even at his mature age, he does not yet seem to have reached the top in his sport – he still brings excitement to the distance running scene, and always with a smile, even after 42,195km.

Following his victory in the 35th real,- Berlin Marathon

Photo Credits

Cover design:	Sabine Groten, Aachen
Cover photo:	Imago Sportfotodienst
Jacket photos:	Klaus Weidt (1)
	Wolfgang Weising (2), Klaus Weidt (1), laurel wreath [iStockphoto] Thinkstock
Page 150:	Map of Ethiopian Airlines (edited);
Interior Pages:	Wolfgang Weising (Pages 100, 134, 135, 136 top, 138, 170), Haile Gebrselassie, private archives (15, 42, 81, 171), Europäischer Buchklub (17), Tourism Commission Ethiopia (25, 76, 96 bottom, 111), Jürgen Pröhl (28, 30), Film "Endurance" (32, 36, 47), "Moskwa 80" (34 bottom), Guide Äthiopien (35, 71), Lutz Brauch (39), "Ethiopian Selamta" (44, 46, 50, 51, 52, 54 top, 58), Film "Revealed" (72, 112, 114 top), Manfred Steffny (85), DPA (132, 133), Bongarts (52), Dubai Marathon office (127), "Laufzeit" 12/10, Victah Seiler (149). All other photos by Klaus Weidt.
Page 62:	clef [Hemera] Thinkstock
Page 88:	hour glass [iStockphoto] Thinkstock
Pages 151-163:	laurel wreath [iStockphoto] Thinkstock

The Gebrselassie family 2008: Haile (with graduation cap), his wife Alem, his three daughters and his son.

Jeff Galloway

HALF-MARATHON

You Can Do It

If you are thinking about training for a half-marathon, Jeff Galloway can help you prepare well, enjoy the training and glow from the achievement of crossing the finish line. The book is loaded with tips on how to stay motivated and eliminate aches, pains, and injuries.

3rd edition, 216 p., full-color print
33 photos, 11 charts, Paperback, 6 1/2" x 9 1/4"
ISBN: 9781841261904
$ 16.95 US/$ 29.95 AUS/£ 12.95 UK/€ 16.95

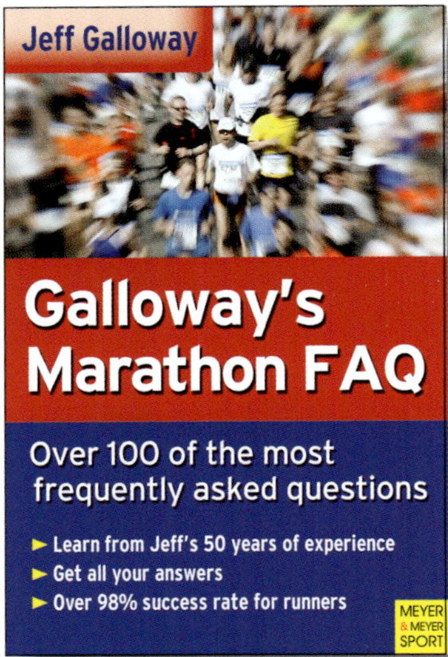

Jeff Galloway

GALLOWAY'S MARATHON FAQ

This book has the direct answers to the most frequently asked questions about training for and running a marathon. Answers are loaded with practical information based upon the overwhelming success that Jeff has had in giving advice during his 35+ years of coaching.
200 p., full-color print, 41 photos, 14 illustrations
Paperback, 6 1/2" x 9 1/4"
ISBN: 9781841262666
$ 17.95 US/$ 29.95 AUS/£ 12.95 UK/€ 16.95

Paul Van Den Bosch

MARATHON

From Beginner to Finisher

Many chase the dream of finishing a marathon one day. Participating in your first marathon demands long, progressive and almost professional preparation. This book is here to help you reach your goal, to become a full-fledged runner and successfully start and finish a marathon.

200 p., full-color print, 35 photos, 36 illustrations
Paperback, 6 1/2" x 9 1/4"
ISBN: 9781841262079
$ 17.95 US/$ 29.95 AUS/£ 12.95 UK/€ 16.95